Fortune favors the
prepared mind...

Louis Pasteur

TRAINING YOUR CREATIVE MIND

Arthur B. VanGundy

BEARLY LIMITED · BUFFALO, NEW YORK

Training Your Creative Mind
by Arthur B. VanGundy, Ph.D.

Second Edition

Address inquiries to Bearly Limited, 149 York Street, Buffalo, New York 14213.

Printed in the United States of America

ISBN 0-943456-36-3

Library of Congress Cataloging in Publication Data
VanGundy, Arthur B.
Training your creative mind.

Bibliography: p. 188.
Includes index.
1. Creative ability – Problems, exercises, etc.
2. Creative thinking – Problems, exercises, etc.
I. Title
BF408.V25 1991

Contents

Acknowledgements

Many thanks go to all the people whose participation in classes and seminars and whose comments, feedback and sample responses to many of the exercises helped me refine and streamline the exercises. I'm also indebted to my copy editor, Candice Egan. Finally, a special note of thanks to Ang Biondi for encouraging and supporting all of my writings on creativity.

Dedication

To Donna and Steven.

Preface

Feel better! Get thinner! Smell nicer! See more clearly! Gain more control over your life!

Sound all too familiar? After being so inundated with virtually hour-by-hour advertisements that are "guaranteed" to "miraculously" help us accomplish one or all of the above goals, you might wonder how, in centuries past, the human race managed to survive without these self-improvement aids.

We seem to have embarked on an endless quest to better ourselves and our lives, trying one tool after another in the hopes of finding that (yet undefined) state of nirvana. And the subject of CREATIVITY has been added to that long list of diets and pep pills, exercise and quit-smoking aids, and subliminal message cassette tapes.

During the last thirty to forty years, there have been hundreds of studies on CREATIVITY and thousands of individuals or groups or organizations have used formal methods to enhance it. It's certainly clear that this interest is not a passing fad.

Although sometimes treated as a fad, it's clear that CREATIVITY is the one "self-improvement aid" we can't do without. The success or failure of all such aids mentioned before initially depended solely on someone's CREATIVITY: the idea for the product itself, the marketing concept, the target audience. All these were (according to your perception) wonderful ways to make lots of money, gain fame, become a highly-credible source of knowledge.

And you and I? Well, we may not at the moment be independently wealthy because we created an astounding new way to lose forty-two pounds in sixteen hours, but most (if not all) of our personal accomplishments have depended upon our creative skills. In a constantly changing environment, it's become absolutely vital to our progress (and maybe even our very survival) to develop new approaches to solving those same old problems that faced daddy and grandma and great-great-uncle Harvey, and creative new ways to overcoming the obstacles we encounter today that would have made the old folks go white with shock.

Assuming you haven't been living in a sound-proof and newspaper-free tunnel for the last several years, you've no doubt noticed that many business and political leaders have jumped on the CREATIVITY bandwagon. It's all around you: you hear the word "innovative" so often lately that you wonder who's the smart guy that created it who's making tons of money in royalties every time it's used.

Given the new spurt of self-help literature and success stories available to us, it's truly a wonder there hasn't been a surfeit of budding Mozarts or Einsteins walking around dressed in the humble trappings of your trash collector, bus driver, or overnight-mail delivery person.

But therein lies the answer and the problem. Multiple reincarnations of Mozart and Einstein may have to wait until the "get-rich-quick" business and political types stop giving lip-service to the concepts of CREATIVITY and start showing us the concrete, practical ways we individually can harness and channel the creative instincts inherent within ourselves.

It's sort of like hiring a builder to construct a house, but failing to provide the blueprints. He wouldn't know where to start or how high to make the walls or if the house was going to be square or circular. Or asking a chef to prepare an elaborate gourmet meal without the benefit of a stove, chopping board or spices.

You've got to have the right tools to accomplish the task. You've got to have a plan. That's what this book is for. In it you'll find a plan and some tools designed to help you grow and function creatively. It's a how-to book that actually will show you how to.

You are obviously a reader who is seriously interested in creative growth. If you weren't, you wouldn't have purchased this book or have read up to this point. What you will find in the pages that follow is a program that will teach you how to correct the imbalance that exists in most of our thinking processes.

You've heard the expression, "I followed my heart instead of my head." In that one phrase is the suggestion that there are two different ways to consider an issue, make a decision, solve a problem. You can "use your head," – a "left-brain" thought process that involves calculation, logic, past experiences. Or you can "go by your heart," – using your "right brain" feelings, instincts, or creativity to come up with an idea that nobody has ever thought of before, and which is so unusual that it just might work.

Both of these thought-processes are important and necessary, but we have been trained from childhood to neglect our creativity in favor of logic. "Stay within the lines when you color," the kindergarten teacher says to the youngster. But what would have happened if the child had been encouraged to color outside of the lines on the drawing? The implication is obvious: if you stay inside the lines and rules and regulations of logical thinking, you're suppressing your creative urges.

As you read on, you'll learn about the general nature of individual creativity, the human mind and brain, distinctions between left and right brain functions, and obstacles to creative thinking. There are exercises for you to do and a program for you to follow, including these details:

- assessing your current level of creative thinking and your readiness to begin the program.
- preparing and carrying out your program.
- your mental attitude, the need for relaxation and some relaxation methods.
- guidelines for evaluating and maintaining training performance.
- exercises on problem preparation, sensory awareness, fluency, originality, evaluation and selection of solutions, and gaining acceptance.

As you progress through the exercises and get into the core of your program, I hope you'll enjoy it and receive as much benefit and pleasure from it as I have received in compiling and writing the program for you.

And when you've finished the book and have glimpsed the exciting, unpredictable world of creative thinking, when you have learned how to make that world a part of your daily life, and when you begin to reap the benefits that result from creative functioning, then the book will have accomplished its objective.

You will have learned how much fun it is to color outside of the lines.

1

Introduction To Mind Training

What percent of the general population do you consider to be creative? Ten percent? Twenty? Thirty? Forty? Fifty percent or more? When I ask this question in workshops and classes, most people select twenty percent or less. Their reasoning seems to be that creativity, like intelligence or other personality attributes, is normally distributed throughout the population. That is, most people are "average" in creativity, while only a small percentage can be considered truly creative or noncreative.

If this assumption is correct, what is it that separates the average from the highly creative people? Why were da Vinci, Franklin and Einstein regarded as creative while others were not? Are the differences hereditary? Or are they due to environmental, social or cultural factors?

The correct answer is that one hundred percent of people in the general population are creative. *All of us are creative; we vary only in the extent to which we have developed our creativity potential.*

The Einstein's and da Vinci's and other people like them somehow managed to grasp the significance of their creativeness and to direct it into channels that brought recognition to their achievements. They learned to maximize their innate creative potential – a potential that exists within every individual.

Throughout our lives, we have been taught and have learned how to be logical and analytical. Most of us have yet to learn how to use our inborn intuitive and creative capabilities. We need to learn how to unlock the creative side of our brain.

Our creative minds were not always locked. As children, we were all capable of developing insights and ideas which, if polished by experience and technical knowledge, would have been considered creative if they had been the ideas of adults. But having been taught, as we grew up, to color within the lines, the creative side of our minds began to atrophy before we ever reached adulthood.

Socrates noted, "That which is used strengthens and grows, while that which is not used withers and dies." It's like a weight lifter who concentrates on building the strength within his left arm while neglecting the right. Over time, the left arm will develop a disproportionate strength far exceeding that of the right.

So it is with our creative minds. To become fully functioning human beings, we must exercise *both* sides of our minds. To deny our creative side is to deny ourselves and our potential to grow to the fullest extent of which we are capable.

We live in a society where cultural values and mores stress conformity and rationality. Independent thinking and creativity are assigned less-important roles. In order to awaken our creative selves, we need to learn to use the neglected right side of our brain, the creative side.

THE HUMAN MIND AND BRAIN

How do the mind and the brain differ? We need to understand this before we can begin to unlock our creative minds.

Although the terms 'mind' and 'brain' are often used synonymously, a rather strict distinction exists between the mind and the brain, especially in terms of how each functions.

The human mind is generally considered to be the center of all mental activity. Through the mind we reason, learn, perceive, judge, feel and perform all the other activities associated with mental functioning. It gives meaning to life and enables us to understand and deal with the world around us.

The mind – not the brain – is intangible. We can't touch it but we know it's there. But the reason why we know the mind is there is because we have a mind. The proof of its existence is in its existence. I think, therefore I am.

The mind cannot be measured or weighed and is not easily subject to scientific scrutiny. It can be tested philosophically but not scientifically, since there is no valid way to measure the scientific existence of the mind and its nature and composition.

In contrast, the brain is an anatomical part of the body. It has size, shape, texture, color, weight and structure. Its effect on other bodily functions can be determined and alternative hypotheses can be developed and scientifically tested to explain such effects. For example, a lesion can be made in the occipital lobe of the brain and observed for its effect on vision. If lesions made on other portions of the brain produce no effect on vision, it then can be concluded that only the occipital lobe is concerned with vision. No such experiments can be conducted on the mind with the same scientific precision.

Although the mind depends on the physical structures of the brain for its existence (providing the organization and connections among the different brain areas that permit discussion of the mind as a concept), the mind is still a philosophical or psychological concept, rather than physiological.

The human brain is thought to have evolved from three different brain forms: reptilian, mammalian and neocortex. The reptilian or first form of the brain contained the stem and neural fibers organized to deal with routine situations. Although still with us, it's not very helpful in making adaptations or dealing with novel situations.

The mammalian brain, as it evolved, became integrated with and surrounded the reptilian brain, and with it we became more adept at such actions as learning, expressing emotions, sensing and responding to environmental changes. It is from this brain that we developed the fight-or-flight response to stressful situations.

The neocortex, in contrast to the two previous brain systems, which integrated their functions, has retained a separate identity. It has provided us with the ability.to speak, think, walk, use symbols, and create. Further evolutionary forms may not be necessary, for we now possess problem solving abilities: we can learn to deal with or adapt to most situations we encounter.

Little is known about how the brain helps us to solve problems. We do know that considerable neuronal activity is involved and that it occurs at an extremely rapid rate – much like but many times faster than a computer. Yet many of the specific chemical processes and centers related to problem solving have continued to elude us. We seem to be limited in our ability to study the brain, perhaps because the brain itself is our major tool for studying it.

TWO BRAINS ARE BETTER THAN ONE

The human brain actually consists of two brains in one, a left and a right hemisphere that are symmetrical in shape but not in function. The left hemisphere controls the right side of the body and vice versa. For example, an injury to the left side of the brain could seriously impair the use of the right arm.

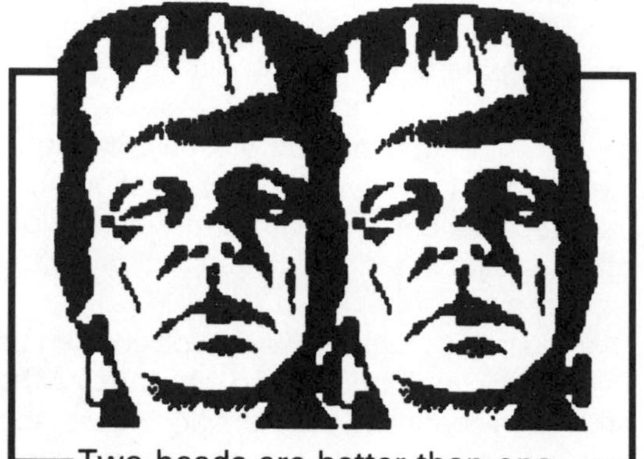
Two heads are better than one.

This distinction between the two hemispheres has been recognized for many years. More recent studies, however, have identified the roles played by the hemispheres in our mental processes, where each half determines how we use our minds.

The left hemisphere is primarily concerned with verbal skills, words, logic and sequence. It processes only one bit of information at a time. In contrast, the right half deals with sensory images and intuition. It sifts through information that cannot be expressed in words, thinks in terms of whole patterns even when only partial information is available, and uses no particular order for processing the information (See Figure 1.1).

Both of these functional distinctions are vital to creative thought. Creative thinking involves manipulation of both words and images. Our creative potential can be maximized only if we utilize both thinking modes, only at different times during the thinking process. Specifically, the right brain helps us avoid rigid, linear thinking so we can concentrate on developing ideas, and the left brain enables us to evaluate the ideas and test them against reality.

Much of our knowledge is the result of the left brain's ability to translate creative insights into words, the symbols we use to communicate and understand ideas. Most creative breakthroughs were not developed singularly through verbal and analytical thinking, but evolved instead from the right brain's ability to image and construct whole patterns and spatial relationships.

Figure 1.1 Comparison of left and right brain hemispheres.

Left Brain	Right Brain
logical	intuitive
sequential	nonsequential
analytical	nonanalytical
rational	emotional
uses words	uses images
systematic	disorderly
intellectual	experiential
literal meanings	metaphorical meanings
objective	subjective
judgmental	nonjudgmental
requires all data	uses incomplete data
realistic	fantasy-like
verbal relations	spatial relations
part-by-part analysis	holistic analysis

Albert Einstein described the two stages of his thought processes. First, he played with different combinations of problem elements without regard to any logical pattern. Here he relied primarily upon the right brain. In the second stage he used his left brain to translate his final solution into conventional words or symbols. Given the magnitude of his achievements, he appears to have made optimal use of both his brain hemispheres.

Both hemispheres must work in harmony if we are to produce creative solutions to our problems. There are times when functioning of one hemisphere must diminish in order to allow the other to accomplish its task. For most of us, achieving a balance between our right and left brains is not a simple matter of switching to the appropriate hemisphere. We need to learn how to awaken our largely under-utilized right brain.

TRAINING YOUR MIND

Developing the creative side of ourselves requires training our minds, just as athletes train and condition their bodies. We must work continually on our ability to confront and deal with the daily problems we face, to strengthen our weak areas and upgrade our strong ones.

We receive practice in these skills every day, constantly being challenged by events that exercise both our creative and analytical minds. In writing a paper, balancing a budget, or interacting with other people we are using both sides of our brains to some extent. Since most of this practice involves the left-brain, that side has become dominant in our thinking.

It is possible to become focused in our approach to which thinking mode is best for a situation. If a task involves developing a new project, we can begin by concentrating on visual images while suspending all logical thinking. Once we have crystalized our approach, we can apply the critical censors of the left brain to evaluate the result. In this manner, we make a conscious attempt to involve the right brain while learning how to integrate it with the left.

We become more disciplined in our approach through practice exercises geared to left or right brain functioning. It is best to begin with exercises designed to strengthen and develop the right, or creative, side of our mind, in order to combat the overpowering influence of our left brains.

The approach for right-brain development should be systematic. Just like you couldn't run a marathon without prior training, so you cannot immediately begin with complex right-brain exercises. The program will have you start out slowly, gradually experiencing different types and intensities of right-brain functioning.

KNOW YOUR PROBLEMS

Most human activity involves problem solving, which requires both logical and creative thinking. Anything we can do to increase our thinking capabilities should help us become better problem solvers.

Problems vary in the type of thinking required to solve them. Although an oversimplification, it can be said that structured problems require mostly left-brain thinking and unstructured, right-brain functioning. The underlying objective of this training program is to increase your ability to solve unstructured problems.

EXPECTATIONS

When we begin anything new, we usually have expectations about what we hope to accomplish, as you no doubt have expectations about how you will be different after completing the program in this book. In addition, I have some expectations for what I hope you will achieve. Any results you or I may expect could be realistic or unrealistic. However, it is important that we are aware of the objectives we have set for ourselves. Such objectives help determine the benefits from what we attempt. If you have not yet assessed your expectations, the space below is provided for you to do that, before proceeding.

____

____

____

____

____

My expectation for you is that you become aware of the power residing in your right brain, develop the ability to apply appropriately this power to the problems you face, and do so as naturally and easily as you already do with your analytical mind.

Of course, just reading this book will not accomplish that. You'll need to experience and understand the exercises presented. Don't just go through the motions. Commit yourself to applying what you learn in order to draw automatically upon both of your brains. Without this commitment, your left brain may resume dominance and prevent your right brain from doing all it can for you.

There are also some specific objectives for you to achieve. After you have finished your training program, your thinking ability should have increased in four major creativity areas: problem sensitivity, flexibility, fluency and originality.

Problem sensitivity is your ability to identify your problems and how their various aspects relate to one another. Flexibility is the skill to break away from conventional problem solving restraints, test surface assumptions and develop new problem perspectives. Fluency enables you to generate many ideas and see different associations and patterns; and originality is the uniqueness of those ideas.

Although the exercises cover many related areas, these four are essential to developing your creative mind. And, since effective problem solving involves both creative and analytical thinking, several of the exercises emphasize the use of the former along with the latter.

Obstacles To Creative Thinking

(I would suggest you read this chapter at least twice, skimming over it first and then rereading for understanding. You'll benefit more from the exercises in later chapters if you develop a keen personal awareness about these obstacles. If possible, try to relate a personal problem to each of the obstacles.)

While I was in high school, I was a member of the track team. My specialty was running the high hurdles, and I had excellent form and style. Unfortunately for me, however, it was speed and not form that won the races. While I was practically a picture of perfection as I sailed across the hurdles, I wasn't very fast.

No matter how hard I worked at it, I couldn't increase my speed beyond a certain point. This was a limitation I had to accept as long as I was part of the team.

Similarly, in creative thinking, you'll likely encounter obstacles from within yourself in addition to some imposed on you externally. But, as in running high hurdles in track, you can learn to identify the obstacles (fix your eyes upon the hurdle) and accept your limitations in dealing with them (your form or speed). In so learning, the obstacles that might have blocked your creative thinking then will become simple hurdles for you to clear.

The track athlete trains for hurdling by first working on form, including proper physical conditioning and the right moves to accomplish the race. Once form is mastered, the next step is to learn how to run over the hurdles. These are right-brain activities that require visualization and practice until the flow and rhythm to clear the hurdles successfully have been developed.

Right-brain activities also are key in creative thinking. After you have identified the obstacles, you need to practice your form – your mental attitudes and skills – in clearing them. Running over the thinking obstacles comes next, where you learn to develop a flow and rhythm and to make adjustments for dealing with each hurdle as you encounter it.

When you develop your own program (described in Chapter 3), the style and form you use to run the creativity race will be considerably different from other people. Because you are unique, you'll have some specific obstacles to overcome that other people might not have. The program will help you develop your own personal internal climate that will allow you to deal with the obstacles on an on-going basis instead of with short-term, one-shot attempts. As in athletic training, if you want to become an Olympian athlete of creativity, you will have to practice continuously.

WHAT ARE THE CREATIVE-THINKING OBSTACLES?

Previously identified by a number of writers (e.g., Adams, 1979), creative-thinking obstacles can be grouped into five major categories: perceptual, emotional, cultural, environmental, and intellectual/expressive. (See Figure 2.1) Because each of the obstacles within the categories affects each individual differently, they are not presented in any particular order and there may be considerable overlapping among the categories.

Each obstacle can be classified as being either internal or external. Internal ones are barriers we impose upon ourselves or have internalized as a result of our developmental experiences. Heredity also may have played a role in the emergence of internal obstacles. External obstacles exist outside of ourselves, such as other people's opinions or perceptions.

To understand the difference between internal obstacles and those that are external, study the diagram in Figure 2.2. At the core of the figure, the three categories of internal obstacles (perceptual, emotional and intellectual/expressive) strongly overlap each other. This suggests much interdependence and commonality. For example, how you function intellectually at any given time is strongly influenced by your emotional climate at that moment.

The core is an immediate subset of the environmental obstacles which, in turn, are a subset of cultural ones. Although not shown, the circles that would represent the obstacles within each of the external categories would also overlap. Thus, factors in the environment may affect things in the culture. Autocratic bosses (environ-

Figure 2.1 Creative thinking obstacles.

Perceptual Obstacles

1. Using overly-restrictive problem boundaries.
2. Inability to isolate the problem.
3. Ignoring familiar sensory inputs (saturation).
4. Stereotyping.
5. Functional myopia.
6. Failure to use all the senses.
7. Difficulty in seeing remote relationships.

Emotional Obstacles

1. Feeling overwhelmed by the problem.
2. Fear of failure.
3. Fear of criticism.
4. Fear of taking a risk.
5. Desire to succeed too quickly.
6. Low tolerance of ambiguity.
7. Failure to incubate.
8. Failure to suspend judgment.

Intellectual/Expressive Obstacles

1. Failure to use an appropriate problem solving language.
2. Use of rigid problem solving strategies.
3. Lack of information or use of incorrect information.

Cultural Obstacles

1. Taboos.
2. Tradition.
3. Lack of a questioning attitude.
4. Over-emphasis on competition or cooperation.
5. Over-emphasis on reason and logic.
6. Belief that fantasy and intuition are a waste of time.
7. Lack of humor.

Environmental Obstacles

1. Lack of time.

2. Lack of support.
3. Distractions.
4. Autocratic bosses.
5. Over-reliance on experts.

---

mental) could greatly reduce a questioning attitude in their employees (cultural). Bosses who make decisions without employee input (environmental) may severely curtail curiosity (cultural). "Just do what you're told and don't ask any questions."

The internal obstacles are shown at the core of the diagram because they are the ones that will exert greater influence over your individual creativity. Once you have learned to liberate your mind and set the stage for unleashing your creative potential, you'll be better able to deal with the external obstacles, because you will have more self-awareness and control over the events in your creative life.

Figure 2.2 Internal and external creative thinking obstacles.

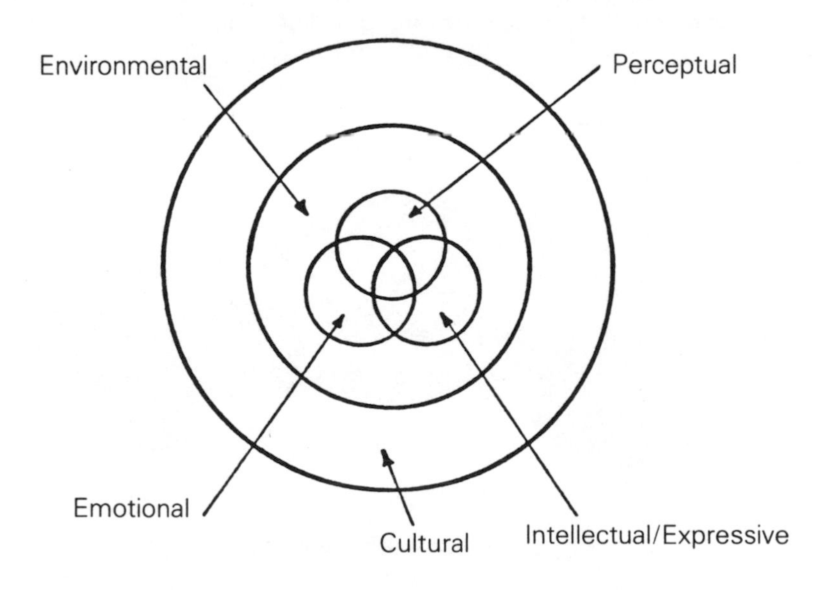

PERCEPTUAL OBSTACLES

1. *Using overly restrictive problem boundaries.* Human beings have a tendency to impose too many constraints on a problem or to impose some that don't exist. If you were trying to develop a new type of lawn mower, you first would have to identify your problem. Does a conventional lawn mower need improving or should you be looking for a new way to maintain grass height at a specified height? Perhaps the solution would be a chemical to retard the growth of the grass. This problem needed to be broadened, or the constraints removed from it.

The reverse also can be true. Some problems may be unnecessarily broad and need to be reduced in scope. Thus, if you are a manufacturer of lawn mowers, you would be restricted to nonchemical solutions due to the constraints imposed by your available technology and equipment. A clear understanding of problem boundaries is essential for effective problem solving.

2. *Inability to isolate the problem.* This deals with adequately defining the problem before you attempt a solution. If your car doesn't start in the morning, you may want to check the gas tank before you begin taking apart the carburetor (correctly solving the wrong problem). You also don't want to fill the gas tank with milk to get the car started (incorrectly solving the right problem).

My car doesn't start very well.

3. *Ignoring familiar sensory inputs (saturation).* Without looking, draw the face of your watch, or a telephone dial with all the letters and numbers in their correct place. Most people are unable to do either of these drawings correctly. That's because the mind retains such data only for a relatively short period of time. It subconsciously ignores most data that have become familiar sights, and no longer recognizes them as novel stimuli. Although this function prevents us from being overwhelmed by minutia or unnecessary information, it can be a disadvantage for creative thinking. To be creative, we need to look at the world with a fresh eye and sense familiar things in a different way, opening up all of our senses and developing new and unique perspectives.

4. *Stereotyping.* To some extent, all of us tend to see what we expect to see. We disregard or reinterpret many facts to conform with our preconceived beliefs. We persist in believing something to be so even when there is little evidence to support our beliefs. This view allows us to create order out of chaos and to deal with ambiguous situations.

However, stereotyping acts as a block to creative thinking. It's difficult to remove a label we have affixed to something. Have you ever given up in frustration when you needed to fix a mechanical device and you didn't have a screwdriver? But if you had not stereotyped the coins in your possession as money, you might have used them to turn the screw. On a more personal level, think of the different ways people have stereotyped you. So many human resources go unused because of the stereotyping we all practice.

In problem solving, we often superficially examine a problem, stereotype it as similar to a previous problem and try to apply the same solution we used before. Again using the analogy of a car, the knocking noise you hear when you drive might not mean a problem with the pistons and the rods. Your seat belt might be hanging outside the car door. Therefore, if you stereotype the problem as similar to the piston problem you had last week, you would take the car for an unnecessary trip to the mechanic. Transferring solutions in this manner can make some problems more difficult to solve, or create entirely new problems. It would have cost much less to restore the seat belt to its correct position.

5. *Functional myopia.* This is a psychological term that describes the tendency to select aspects of a problem related to your training in a certain discipline. We usually describe organizational problems from the perspective of our own department. The assembly-line worker is concerned with on-the-job safety, the recruiter with hiring and turnover of personnel, and the financial officer with cash flow. If asked to describe the most pressing problem facing their company, each of these individuals would invariably reply in terms of their own functional areas.

Viewing a complex, unstructured problem (i.e., one with many interdependent parts) from only one perspective is not likely to produce a unique or effective solution. We need to consider how people in another discipline might solve the problem. In addition, if you ask people from different areas for their opinion, you're likely to enrich your knowledge and increase your problem-solving odds.

6. *Failure to use all the senses.* Although we are continually bombarded by a variety of sensory inputs – sounds, textures, colors, flavors, odors – we rarely make full use of all our senses in solving problems. We have become conditioned to using verbal skills, a left-brain activity.

Stop and smell the flowers.

Many businesses, fast-food restaurants for example, capitalize on this tendency we have to ignore the interrelation of our senses. Notice how many interiors in such restaurants use shades of orange, gold, brown and red. These colors are proven appetite stimulants. A national pizza franchise had a location in a highly-populated and travelled area. This location, however, was forced to close operations because of lack of business. The interior of that particular restaurant was decorated in cool shades of blue and green.

Effective problem-solving requires that we consider our problems in as many ways as possible. To avoid approaching our problems from too narrow a perspective, we need to open up the sensory grab bag that exists in us all.

7. *Difficulty in seeing remote relationships.* Most creative thought involves making connections between apparently unrelated ideas. To avoid traditional, mundane solutions, we must learn to see the similarities or differences between objects or ideas. If we use only judgment and logic to obtain our ideas, we restrict the number of solution possibilities as well as the uniqueness of the final solution.

What association might wet leaves have with potato chips? Although it's difficult to make this association, it was noted that wet leaves become easily compressed when they are wet. By adding water and compressing dehydrated potatoes, almost any form can be produced. That was the beginning of potato chips made from dehydrated potatoes. A once-difficult association becomes easy once the dominance of the left brain is overcome.

EMOTIONAL OBSTACLES

1. *Feeling overwhelmed by the problem.* Unstructured problems provide few guidelines for solutions and usually consist of many sub-problems. This can lead to feeling overwhelmed and under stress as we attempt to solve the large problem.

A realistic approach is to develop a systematic process to break down the problem into more manageable units. Thus, the enormity of the problem won't be so overpowering. An office manager faced with the task of increasing office efficiency (an overwhelming problem) would have to deal separately with, perhaps, the workers' schedules, the outdated photocopier, a streamlined office design (manageable units). Before a complex problem can be resolved, the problem of *how* to go about solving it must first be tackled. Once you've done this, the emotional obstacle presented by an originally overwhelming problem is greatly diminished.

2. *Fear of failure.* Many people, especially those who are determined to succeed at everything they do, react with considerable anxiety to life's *unpredictability.* What if their endeavors result in failure? Some people even fail to try because they are so worried about failing.

Although it would be nice if we could predict the outcome of every one of our actions, variables unknown to us or beyond our control will always affect outcomes. But a basic fact of life is that most people who have succeeded in life have done so with the *benefit* of their failures. They used them as stepping-stones to success.

A staff accountant once made a significant business contact for her company at a party she attended. The next morning she excitedly related the specifics to her manager, expecting him to praise her achievement. Instead, he rather coldly informed her that business development was his job, not hers. What made her think the firm would even consider accepting the new client she recommended? Although the accountant might have stopped there, viewing the whole experience as a failure, she took steps to set up a meeting between her manager and the senior executives of the potential client company. Although her manager at first resisted, the meeting resulted in a highly lucrative account for the firm and an early promotion for the accountant.

3. *Fear of criticism.* This obstacle could fit well in either the emotional or cultural categories. Human nature – because many people cannot tolerate the thought of change – and our culture are both inclined toward negative criticism of new ideas. Expected negative criticism can cause us as individuals to shy away from presenting anything new or radical. Thus, probably thousands of valuable ideas have been lost to the world.

Allowing the emergence of creative thought requires a climate of openmindedness. Even if the new idea proves to be an unworkable one, when you practice a willingness to change the status quo, the original idea could lead to one that does work.

4. *Fear of taking a risk.* We've been taught from childhood that the safe course is the easy course: look before you leap, take it easy, put safety first. Granted, such caution plays an important part in helping us avoid situations that could jeopardize our lives, careers, or marriages.

However, in creative problem solving, the opposite attitude is needed. Innovative ideas would never have come about if their creators all had been concerned with whether the general public would like instant oatmeal, or if the new engine might require too much steel, or if the airplane would create sonic booms. You'll never propose or accept a new idea if you allow yourself to be hindered by the results you imagine it causing.

5. *Desire to succeed too quickly.* Our society greatly reinforces doing things to the best of our abilities. Aggressively tackling a project, giving it all you've got, is the way to get ahead.

Sometimes, though, we simply try too hard, becoming so motivated that we end up performing below our actual capabilities. When I was running the hurdles in high school, I often became so strained and tense that I actually ran slower. Once I relaxed, I was able to increase my time over the hurdles so that I at least looked like I was running fast in slow motion.

Look before you leap.

Leaping into problem-solving with the expectation of a quick solution is likely to produce just that: a quick, but not a well-thought out or unique and workable solution. Some time needs to be spent analyzing your problem, in incubating – which is the unconscious digestion of ideas. Your left brain urges you toward immediate resolution. Unless you allow your right brain time to mull over the problem, you won't find a creative solution.

6. *Low tolerance of ambiguity.* People who have trouble tolerating uncertainty often think in "either-or" terms; they have a strong desire for closure. Things are never gray to them; it's either right or wrong, black or white, smart or dumb, happy or sad. They want to rush right in and solve problems without bothering to define the situation. The solution is more important than the problem.

The ability to bring order out of chaos has a definite place in our society. The difficulty arises when such people apply creative thinking to unstructured problems. The problem is very fuzzy to these individuals, and thus very frustrating, so they look for a quick fix or speedy solution. Problem-solving does involve elements of restoring order, but an overemphasis on this won't produce satisfactory results.

7. *Failure to incubate.* Incubation is a right-brain, unconscious activity that occurs following a period of intense concentration and when

Incubation is not always easy.

we have left the problem to do something unrelated. Then, when we least expect it, we suddenly hit upon a solution or an alternative approach. It is the "aha!" experience frequently reported by people who have developed creative insights to their problems.

Failure to incubate becomes an obstacle when you don't provide enough time away from your problem to allow your right brain to digest it. This time-out could be as little as twenty minutes or, for more complex issues, several days or weeks.

Depending on the school of thought, incubation results from (1) a realization that followed a long period of problem saturation; (2) encountering new information that helped provoke new ideas, or (3) removing creative inhibitions caused by a limited perspective or mental fatigue. However it is interpreted, temporarily getting away from a problem can provide conditions which might lead to new problem viewpoints.

8. *Failure to suspend judgment.* This obstacle occurs when we are on the giving end of negative criticism. Even though our society places much emphasis on negative criticism – (for example, in educational institutions and the media) – an overdose of it can be self-defeating. Rejecting an idea as soon as it is proposed is like throwing away flower seeds because they aren't very pretty and we weren't willing to give the seeds the chance to produce beautiful blooms.

Some colleagues and I once experienced this tendency when we proposed that students be exposed to creative-thinking techniques in addition to the heavy doses of analytical thinking that was the norm. The initial reaction was that creativity is something that can't be taught, each person must develop it alone, and there aren't enough resources to facilitate the idea. The officials didn't see one positive feature of the proposal and, while they were busy negating it, one colleague passed me a note. "I think we are talking to the problem."

To avoid becoming part of the problem, we need to examine our behavior when new ideas are presented. Criticism can always come later on, but first we should consider the idea or how it can be combined with other ones.

INTELLECTUAL/EXPRESSIVE OBSTACLES

1. *Failure to use appropriate problem-solving language.* Depending

on the problem that needs to be solved, verbal (left-brain) language can be the wrong language to use when right-brain, or visual, language is required. If you were designing a new car, you would be severely limited if you relied alone upon verbal thinking and neglected visual thinking.

Normally the language we select to solve a problem is an unconscious decision resulting from prior trial-and-error approaches to similar problems. Because most of us are dominated by left-brain thinking, we need to make conscious choices about which problem-solving language should be used.

Consider the following problem: All dogs have fur. This animal has fur. Therefore, it is a dog.

Some people will quickly look at the problem, verbally analyze it and conclude that the last statement is true. However, as seen in Figure 2.3, a Euler diagram, dogs are a subset of animals with fur. Therefore, this animal is not a dog. Although the problem could have been solved using mathematical or verbal skills, the truth of the statement can be tested more easily using a simple diagram.

2. *Use of rigid problem-solving strategies.* This obstacle is similar to the previous one. We often become blocked by an inability to switch from one problem-solving process to another, using mathematics, for example, when such a solution isn't possible. An old riddle illustrates this point.

Farmer John's will provided for each of his three sons to inherit a different number of the seventeen horses left on the farm. The oldest son would receive half, the second son a third of the horses, and the youngest would get one-ninth. The will stipulated that none of the horses was to be killed to satisfy the requirements. How was the will carried out?

The problem could not be solved mathematically, because the fractions do not add up to the whole. A possible solution would be for the brothers together to buy another horse. The provisions of the will could then be carried out with *eighteen* horses. The point here is that a solution other than mathematics had to be found.

3. *Lack of information or use of incorrect information.* "A little knowledge is a dangerous thing." This maxim is certainly true in many situations. If you wanted to rewire an electrical system in a house,

Figure 2.3 Example of a Euler diagram.

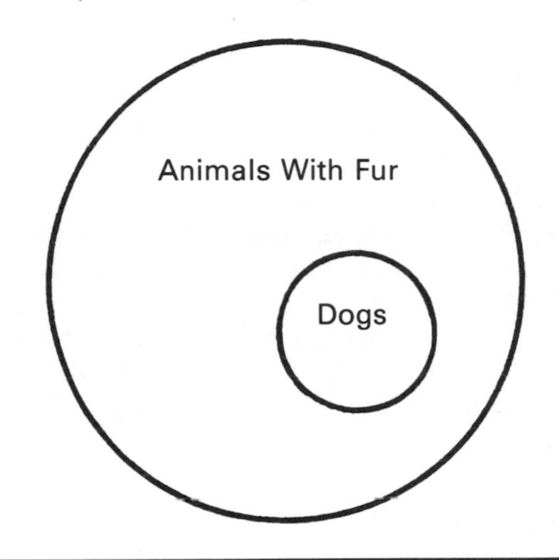

you would have to know more than the basics, or you'd end up frying yourself.

In creative problem solving, though, having a little knowledge is good. If you had too much information, you might not develop new problem viewpoints. With only a little knowledge, you won't be likely to use preconceived notions about how to produce solutions. You'll know just enough about the problem to play around with ideas but not enough to approach it with blinders on.

Entirely different is using incorrect information. Here it doesn't matter how much information you have because one bit of erroneous information can throw off the entire problem-solving process. The assumptions behind all information must be continually tested to make sure the "real" problem will be solved.

CULTURAL OBSTACLES

1. *Taboos.* Taboos are standards that society imposes upon us to make us think or act certain ways. Most of these have a rational basis for their development. The Jewish taboo against eating pork, for example, originated at a time when cooking standards were not

as safe as they are today; in fact, the Jewish people were protecting themselves from trichinosis.

Taboos become an obstacle when they are used to restrict the range of possible solutions. If our culture does not permit something, we are less likely to consider using it in creative problem solving.

2. *Tradition.* Most traditions are comfortable, secure, and certain. Most change is uncomfortable, threatening and uncertain. Although tradition is a valuable link to understanding the past, many traditions are anathema to creative problem solving. Being too bound by tradition will restrict our solving capabilities, because most creative solutions require some degree of change on the part of others. Change cannot occur unless people are willing to break away from some of their traditions.

3. *Lack of a questioning attitude.* If you rarely ask questions, you rarely risk appearing ignorant. But, you also risk not growing and learning. Children are often admonished to stop asking so many questions. As we grow older, this natural curiosity about everything around us becomes stagnated.

A questioning attitude is essential for all aspects of creative problem solving. You need to gather facts continually about problem situations. Often, the more questions you ask, the easier it will be to develop solutions.

4. *Overemphasis on competition or cooperation.* Although both these traits are healthy components of individual, group and organizational functioning, there is danger when we feel pressed to be too competitive or cooperative. Instead, we may lose sight of the problem we're trying to solve, devoting most of our energies to being first to develop a solution rather than finding the most effective one. Too much cooperation, or a concern about not "rocking the boat," can cause us to rely less on our own uniqueness as creative problem solvers.

5. *Overemphasis on reason and logic.* The use of reason and logic is a left-brain function. Sometimes we tend to rely too much on reason and logic to solve a problem, thus stifling our creative insights. Intuition and feeling, which are right-brain functions, provide new

ways of looking at problems and help us conceptualize unique solutions.

Idle time spent thinking about flying.

6. *Belief that fantasy and intuition are a waste of time.* Our society has taught us to be fact-oriented beings and many of us consider fantasy to be unproductive. There are situations, however, when we must speculate and daydream to allow our right-brains to mull over a problem. How many people do you suppose spent "idle" time dreaming about how humans could fly? If they had not allowed

themselves to dream, we'd be spending a lot more time today in travelling.

7. *Lack of humor.* Like many aspects of human behavior (physical, spiritual, emotional), problem solving is characterized by tension buildup and release. Tension exists when we first are confronted by the mess known as a problem and it increases (or decreases) in accordance with our perception of progress made toward a solution. Viewed this way, problem solving is serious business.

Humor is a form of tension release. Being too serious stifles creativity.

Often a humorous insight involving an illogical concept stimulates a solution. Laughter unlocks some of our rigid thinking patterns and is an excellent way to break out of mental ruts. Perhaps it was a busy 1940's working mother, frustrated by her lack of desire and time to cook, who joked during a cooking class that she wished meals came in boxes. Her classmates probably rolled around in side-splitting laughter, but thus the concept of convenience foods might not have been born.

ENVIRONMENTAL OBSTACLES

1. *Lack of time.* Developing creative solutions to unstructured problems requires considerably more time than solving structured problems to which routine procedures can be applied. Time can be a serious constraint here, but there is also research evidence that having a deadline commitment actually may increase the creativity of the solutions produced. Nevertheless, most problem solvers would be wise to abide by the words of Henry Ford. "The more you think, the more time you have."

2. *Lack of support.* Support is necessary to creative thinking, whether it be physical, monetary, emotional or moral. It provides the minimal conditions needed to conceptualize effectively and is even more crucial when we attempt to put ideas into action. If you wanted to quit your job to become a free-lance artist, you'd need, at the very least, monetary support to live, and emotional support from your family or mate to live in harmony.

3. *Distractions.* Have there been times you wished you were a her-

mit, and did those times coincide with a problem you were trying to solve? Phone calls, other people, noises, smells, sights, and the temperature all are factors that can disrupt our concentration.

Some people can effectively block out distractions, having learned to "turn off their ears," as my daughter Sarah used to say. On the other hand, some distractions might be helpful in problem solving if they are used to stimulate ideas. To a chemist working on a new drug, a ringing telephone could suggest a time-release capsule. But once the stimulation has been achieved, the ringing may be only another distraction to be eliminated.

4. *Autocratic bosses.* Bosses play a critical role in the stimulation of imagination and creative thinking. They set for their employees an atmosphere of cooperation, competition, achievement, conflict, participation, mistrust or any other environmental forces.

Whether the head honcho stresses freedom of thought or only gives lip service to it, that attitude will be communicated and transmitted down through the organization to others.

The amount of emphasis placed on creative thinking in an organization varies with the personalities of the top executives and should mesh with the structure, size, goals and objectives of the organization. Creativity needs to be managed by the bosses, just as they manage any other organizational resource. A severe case of "imarightis" on the part of the boss will inhibit the maximum use of their human resources.

5. *Overreliance on experts.* It is very easy to depend upon others to solve our problems. Although there is nothing wrong with seeking advice from time to time, we must learn to avoid accepting expert opinion at face value. Much of this expert knowledge was gained through a personal interpretation of known or thought-to-be-known facts.

We need to hone our own conceptual skills, distinguish fact from opinion and question the assumptions and motivations of anyone who professes to be an expert.

OVERCOMING CREATIVE-THINKING OBSTACLES

Now that you are aware of the obstacles to creative thinking, it is time to move on toward learning how to overcome or lessen the effect of the obstacles. The program in the next chapters will help you develop the specific attitudes and actions to accomplish this.

Each of us varies considerably in the nature and extent of our creativity blocks; therefore, some aspects of the program may prove easier or harder for you to accomplish than for other people.

Since we are not always aware of how or when we became blocked in problem solving, we need to develop the awareness of which specific obstacles face us, and then determine which ones we can and want to overcome. Use this preparatory exercise: Think about a problem you are trying to solve. After you have worked on it or have resolved it, think back to which obstacles you encountered. Consider which of those you were not able to overcome, how you might do so the next time, and why they caused you trouble. If you do this for several problems, your "obstacle awareness" should increase substantially.

Here are some specific actions and attitudes to consider in overcoming the obstacles:

Perceptual Obstacles

1. Always test all assumptions about problem-boundaries; avoid placing unnecessary constraints on the problem.
2. Search for and isolate the real problem.
3. View the problem in a different way, using a different sense, than you would normally.
4. Avoid prematurely assigning a label to the problem.
5. Consult with others in a different discipline to see how they would solve the problem.
6. Experience the problem as much as possible, considering its taste, texture, smell, sound, or appearance.
7. Associate unrelated objects or ideas to it, looking for similarities and differences.

Emotional Obstacles

1. Break down complex problems into manageable units and only work on one unit at a time.
2. Recognize that failure sometimes comes before success, and that growth comes from learning about our failures.

3. Keep an open mind about possible criticism of your ideas, remembering that all our ideas have value because of our uniqueness.
4. Be prepared to give up a little to get a little by weighing the probable negative consequences of any risk-taking action against no action at all.
5. Practice being patient in problem solving, realizing that you are not just looking for any solution, but for the best solution for your needs.
6. Defer judgment when you begin work on a problem, perhaps by rapidly listing possible solutions and corresponding weaknesses of each. Throw away the list and begin again by redefining the problem.
7. Take time to allow the problem to incubate after a period of intense concentration.
8. Always ask, "What's good about it?" when you consider a new idea, and never reject an idea outright.

Intellectual/Expressive Obstacles

1. Analyze the problem to determine the most appropriate language to use in solving it – verbal, mathematical or visual.
2. Use several problem-solving strategies, not limiting yourself to only one approach.
3. Continually collect information throughout the problem-solving process; ascertain the validity of all information, and separate facts from opinions.

Cultural Obstacles

1. Recognizing the cultural taboos that restrict your view, consider if your rejection is taboo inspired or due to a solution's lack of merit.
2. Break away from some traditions if the risks of doing so are relatively low and the outcome is likely to lead to a solution.
3. Ask as many questions as you can think of about the problem, not fearing to ask "why?" or "why not?"
4. Help ensure that group problem solving retains a problem

orientation without undue emphasis on competition or cooperation.

5. Explore all solutions based on intuition and feeling. And don't be afraid to jump to conclusions after the problem has been defined.
6. Allow yourself the freedom to fantasize and daydream about the problem; try to relate these activities to achieving a feasible solution.
7. Use the problem's humorous aspects to suggest possible solutions.

Environmental Obstacles

1. Use problem-solving procedures to gain more time to work on your problems.
2. Actively solicit support for your efforts by showing others how they might benefit from the solution.
3. Use distractions to suggest possible solutions and then search for ways of eliminating, reducing or accepting the distractions.
4. Learn to live with autocratic bosses, change their behavior or leave the situation, and evaluate the negative consequences of each possible action.
5. Avoid overdependence on experts, testing the rationale or knowledge behind an opinion, seeking to understand "why," and daring to seek second opinions.

Steps To Overcoming Creative-Thinking Obstacles

1. Learn to think positively about the obstacles. Realize that most of them can be overcome or lessened in their effects if you believe they can.
2. Commit yourself to overcoming the obstacles. After reading about them and how to overcome them, practice constantly eliminating them and learning how to experience the sensations that come from overcoming the obstacles.
3. Realize that much patience is required. Most of the thinking obstacles took a long time to develop and emerge. Breakdown of these obstacles will take a long time to accomplish.

Problem solving requires a great deal of perseverance, as does creating the internal and external climates needed to help you become a more creative problem solver. We'll discuss this in depth in the next chapter.

Developing Your Training Program

There are no easy shortcuts for any kind of personal change. Whether training for a career, job skills, athletics or personal development, you need to make considerable investments of time, energy and other personal resources. If you really want to succeed at training, you must commit and persevere to achieving your objectives.

In developing a new way of thinking about and solving problems, you must become an active participant in your own development. Just reading this book and learning by osmosis will not be enough.

You will be more successful in using this program if you adopt a middle-of-the-ground approach – one that has reason and order but is not so confining as to inhibit creativity. Too haphazard an approach will result in a mess of unconnected learnings and experiences; too structured will not give you the flexibility to break away from conventional thought patterns.

The program in this chapter is systematic, with exercises to help you gradually train your creative mind. Although it is not necessary for you to follow any specific sequence, try to progress gradually through the program rather than skipping over the exercises that may seem silly or too easy. (You can return to an exercise if you feel you haven't completed it to the best of your ability.) Even if you have a well-developed right brain, practice is always beneficial in learning something new.

The program is divided into three phases: (1) warm-up, or exercises that require relatively little right-brain effort; (2) intermediate, which requires a greater amount of right-brain functioning, and (3) applied, where you apply what you have learned to a sample program and a personal problem.

All three phases should take about fifteen weeks to complete, but you should continue with the program much longer. Many of the exercises can be repeated with additional benefit as you continue working on various problems in your life.

Before describing the program, you should spend some time developing the appropriate climate within yourself. To do this, you will use right-brain training that involves attitude and awareness levels, and personal assessments.

DEVELOP THE PROPER MENTAL ATTITUDE

The more you expect to become more creative, the more likely it is you will. One way to develop your own self-fulfilling prophecy is to recall the statement made in Chapter 1: we are all creative but we vary in the degree to which we have maximized our potential.

All you have to do is think in terms of becoming more creative, since you already are creative now. You've been creative in the past, in spite of many obstacles. You can continue to develop in this direction by thinking positively about what you want to become.

However, you must begin thinking this way today. Don't put off something as important as your own development.

3.01 LEARN TO RELAX

To assess your mental attitude toward creativity, write down the three most important things you have ever done. Do not include growing up or having children. Instead, focus upon things you have personally done which illustrate your individual creativity.

____

____

____

____

____

The things you listed say something about how you see yourself and your creative potential. For instance, are the things on your list typical of artistic creativity, financial creativity, or day-to-day problem solving? The ease with which you thought of these things also may reveal something about yourself. If you had little trouble thinking of creative things, you probably have a positive attitude about your creativity.

LEARN TO RELAX

Even with the proper mental attitudes, your mind and body must be receptive to change and learning in a right-brain mode. Relaxation exercises can help achieve this receptivity and can rid you, at least temporarily, of various stressors that inhibit your creative-thinking potential. Your overall receptivity to the exercises will be greater if you regularly practice relaxation techniques.

Learn to relax.

One elementary relaxation procedure is to focus on your breathing. First, lie down on the floor on your back or sit in a comfortable chair. Close your eyes and visualize all the tension flowing out. Feel it flow from your feet, legs, stomach, chest, neck and shoulders. Allow several minutes for the tension to flow out, then inhale deeply and hold your breath for five to ten seconds, exhaling vigorously. Continue inhaling and exhaling for at least five minutes. While you do this, focus on the tension that is released each time you exhale. You should become progressively more relaxed each time you expel air. If you don't notice any change, concentrate more or eliminate distractions in your environment.

A more elaborate relaxation method begins by lying down on the floor or a hard bed with your legs uncrossed and your arms at your side. Clench your right fist with ever-increasing tension, being aware how the tension affects your fist, hand and forearm. Relax your fist and feel the tension ebb away. Do the same procedure again and repeat it twice with your left fist, then simultaneously with both fists.

Bend your arms at the elbow and make your biceps as tense as possible, being aware of how tense they have become. Release the tension and straighten your arms, feeling the relaxing sensations. Repeat at least one more time.

Move to your head, wrinkling your forehead as tightly as possible. Relax your forehead and visualize it becoming smooth again. Frown and then relax. Close your eyes and hold them closed very tightly, feeling the tension. Relax the tension around your eyes but allow them to remain closed for a few moments. Now tense your jaw, biting down very hard. Relax. Press your tongue against the roof of your mouth as hard as you can. Allow your tongue to relax. Feel the absence of tension in your forehead, scalp, eyes, jaw and tongue.

Tilt your head back and experience the tension in your neck. Roll your head right and left, noticing how the tension areas change. Relax and press your chin to your chest, feeling the tension in your throat and the back of your neck. Return your head to a comfortable position and release the tension. Feel the muscles in your neck letting go.

Now bend your head forward slightly and bunch up your shoulders, feeling the tension in them build. Relax your shoulders and sense the release spreading through your neck, throat and shoulders.

You should be feeling more and more relaxed now.

Tense your thighs and buttocks. Relax and notice the difference between the states of tension and relaxation. Tense your calves by bending your toes downward. Feel the tension. Now relax. Tighten your shins by curling your toes upward. Relax.

Finally, experience the sense of deep relaxation throughout the lower half of your body. Feel your feet, ankles, calves, shins, knees, thighs and buttocks becoming more and more relaxed. Concentrate on these sensations for a few moments. Then imagine how this relaxed state is spreading up your body, to your stomach, lower back and chest. Let more and more of the tension flow away. Feel the relaxation spreading to your arms, hands and shoulders. Become more and more relaxed. Be aware of how loose and supple all your neck, jaw and facial muscles have become.

You will get more out of this experience if you have someone read the instructions to you or if you record them for playback to yourself. If you tape record the instructions, allow sufficient pauses to experience the tension and relaxation activities.

3.02 ON PURPOSE

Before you assess your creative thinking capabilities, you first should consider your "purpose" in life. What provides your life focus? While we all have different goals, if we become aware of the most important ones, we can assign priorities and be much closer to determining our purpose. To do that, try the following.

1. Write down all the things you value about yourself and find interesting.

2. Write down things you like to do. Which of these do you do well?

3. Review all the information you have recorded so far and identify common areas and give them names (e.g., finances, sports, interpersonal relationships).

4. Use the information within each area to develop purpose statements. Base your statements upon the information. If you have a financial area, you might state, "My purpose is to help people better manage their money." Develop as many statements as you wish.

5. Choose one or more purpose statements which best describe your priorities in life.

This often revealing exercise can help you discover things about yourself you never considered before. If you did not have a positive reaction, you may not have been in a responsive mood and might wish to try again. If you were pleased with the outcome, consider how your purpose relies upon creative abilities. To illustrate, if your purpose is to help others with financial planning, creativity comes into play by just convincing them they need such assistance and devising ways to finance the plan.

ASSESS YOUR CREATIVE-THINKING ABILITIES

The only way you can evaluate a change in yourself is to identify your current level of creative functioning. Once you know where you are, you will be in a better position to successfully move ahead in training your creative mind. One relatively simple rating instrument of your creative problem solving abilities is shown in Figure 3.1 on page 36. Although geared specifically to the exercises in this book, it has no known scientific validity. It can, however, help force you to consider some of the major attributes of creative problem solving, or at least get you thinking about the topic. Complete this instrument before you begin your program. Score yourself by adding up your numerical responses.[1] Then evaluate your responses using the following scale:

15 - 26 Not very capable
27 - 38 Below average
39 - 50 Average
51 - 62 Above average
63 - 75 Exceptionally capable

DETERMINE YOUR CREATIVE READINESS

Readiness in this regard refers to how prepared and motivated you are to undertake the training program, and how predisposed you are to unleash your creative potential.

[1] You might consider consulting one or more of the following instruments for evaluating creative abilities: Torrance Tests of Creative Thinking (Torrance, 1974), How Creative Are You? Instrument (Raudsepp, 1980), and Learning Profile Survey Form [a measure of right- and left-brain dominance] (Hermann, 1980).

Figure 3.1 Creative Problem-Solving Capability Rating Scale.

Instructions: Using the scale that follows, rate yourself on each item according to how capable you believe you are in performing the activity described. When rating yourself on the items, try to think in terms of most problems you have dealt with rather than any particular problem. There are no right or wrong answers and your first reaction is likely to be the best.

1 = Not very capable
2 = Below average
3 = Average
4 = Above average
5 = Exceptionally capable

How capable do you consider yourself to be when it comes to:

1. Analyzing problem situations? ______
2. Being aware of and sensitive to different problem elements? ______
3. Being aware of problem constraints? ______
4. Testing major problem assumptions? ______
5. Using your different senses to help analyze the problem or generate ideas? ______
6. Rapidly generating ideas? ______
7. Deferring judgment when generating ideas? ______
8. Viewing a problem from many different perspectives? ______
9. Making remote associations among problem elements? ______
10. Forcing together two or more ideas or objects to produce something new? ______
11. Seeing something positive in every idea? ______
12. Evaluating and selecting ideas? ______
13. Anticipating possible solution consequences? ______
14. Tolerating ambiguity? ______
15. Gaining acceptance for your ideas? ______

Being creatively capable is not enough to fully develop your right brain; you also must possess the minimal resources and motivation to change yourself. For example, unless you have time to devote to creativity training, you are not likely to achieve very much.

Other types of readiness factors are shown in Figure 3.2, the Creative Thinking Training Readiness Scale. Complete this scale now by rating each factor and adding up the scores to find your total readiness index.

If you score between 40 and 50, you likely are ready to begin your program. A score between 15 and 39 suggests you might want to re-examine those readiness factors that have a low score, to see

---

Figure 3.2 Creative Thinking Training Readiness Scale.

Instructions: Using the following scale, indicate the extent to which each item is a concern to you in regard to your readiness for a creative thinking training program. For example, if you believe that you have plenty of time to devote to such a program, you might give that item a score of "5."

1 = Critical concern
2 = Important concern
3 = Moderate concern
4 = Mild concern
5 = No concern

1. Time availability ______
2. Commitment to becoming more creative ______
3. Your willingness to take risks ______
4. Support (if needed) available to complete the program ______
5. Your willingness to persevere ______
6. Environmental distractions ______
7. Your openness to new experiences ______
8. Your desire to improve yourself ______
9. The extent to which you have clearly defined your life goals and objectives ______
10. Your overall motivation level ______

---

which you might be able to change. Use your intuition, however. Some items you rated low might not significantly deter you.

If you scored 14 or below, you probably need to rethink beginning the program. With such a score, your efforts are likely to be haphazard and show little benefit. However, you may change your mind after beginning or external conditions might vary enough to justify starting the program. You need to consider whether it is best for you to begin and see what happens, or to wait for a few weeks or months to start the program. The key, however, is to re-assess your motivation continually until you feel you can begin comfortably.

DESIGN YOUR PROGRAM

Warm-up. Figure 3.3 shows the suggested exercises for the warm-up phase and the approximate time required or allotted for each. The exercises have been divided into blocks, and you should try to complete each block within one week and in the order presented. Begin with block number one on the bottom row, just as you would start a foundation for a house. Try to average at least ten to fifteen minutes per day for five days each week.

Adjustments may be made if this pace is too slow or fast for you, although you should not try to complete the exercises too slowly or quickly. Doing only one exercise per week, for example, will eliminate the benefits of cumulative learnings; doing the entire phase within one or two weeks will block the incubation that might help you better understand your experience.

Intermediate. The intermediate phase, as seen in Figure 3.4, consists of exercises organized into six blocks with the same average time requirements as the warm-up phase. Again, use your own discretion in varying the amount of time to spend on the exercises, but complete them in sequence because they are organized to progressively refine right-brain skills or degrees of difficulty.

Applied. In this phase, you will try to apply your learnings to a hypothetical situation and then to a personal problem. The hypothetical problem and a sample response are described in Chapter 11.

Tips to consider before you begin your program:

1. Set aside a specific time each day to work on the exercises. If that is not possible, use your spare moments while commuting, waiting in airports, etc. If you do use such locations,

Figure 3.3 Suggested warm-up phase exercises.

I		Time (in minutes)
3.01	Triadic Deeds	5
3.02	On Purpose	10
4.01	Goal Visualization	10
4.02	How Much Are You Worth	10
4.03	Think About It	10
4.11	Good Sense Shopping	5
4.12	Visual Smorgasbord	10
5.01	Your Room	10
5.02	The Picnic	5
5.03	Touch It	5
5.04	I Hear Ya	15
5.11	Brain Vacation	10
5.12	Thoughtful Images	10

II		Time (in minutes)
5.05	Sensory Stretch	5
5.06	Be a Banana	5
5.07	Mowing Along	5
5.13	Working Out	10
6.01	Square Off	5
6.02	Don't Fence Me In	10
6.03	Create a New Viewpoint	5
6.04	Switch Around	2
6.05	Symbol Relatives	10
6.06	Spy Telegrams	5
6.07	Breakdown	20
6.17	Fill 'er Up	3
6.18	Dots the Way	3

III		Time (in minutes)
4.13	Mind Mapping	10
4.14	Name That Letter	5
4.15	Disfigured	3
5.15	Square Search	10
5.16	Tabloid Attention	3
6.08	Take a Stand	5
6.09	Take It Off	5
7.01	Brain Gusher	15
7.02	Prefix-It	5
7.03	Letter Hunt	5
7.04	Underweight	3
7.05	Word Chains	12
7.06	Sniff Out	15

IV		Time (in minutes)
6.16	Cut-Up	10
6.19	Letter Line-Up	5
7.07	Word Relatives	5
8.01	Steaming Ideas	20
8.02	Fill-Out	10
8.03	Draw-A-Word	10
8.04	Picture That	20
8.05	Something New	10

V		Time (in minutes)
8.06	Grid Lock	15
9.01	Values	10
9.02	Wired Up	10
9.03	Light the Way	10
10.01	Idea Garden	15
10.02	Freeze-Unfreeze	15

Figure 3.4 Suggested intermediate phase exercises.

IV	Time (in minutes)	V	Time (in minutes)	VI	Time (in minutes)
5.17 Plane to See	15	9.04 Category Crunch	15	10.04 You Can Take This Job and . . .	45
7.15 Spy Stories	15	9.05 Weigh-in	20	10.05 I Scream	
7.18 Funny Knife	10	9.20 Criteria Cafeteria	20		
8.07 Label It	10	10.03 Consultant	45		
8.08 Light Up Your Life	15				
8.09 Word to Word	15				
8.10 Name That Exercise	15				
8.19 Nova Speak	15				

I	Time (in minutes)	II	Time (in minutes)	III	Time (in minutes)
4.04 Early Bird	10	5.09 Cube Imagery	5	7.08 Gar * bage	15
4.05 Imagine That	5	5.10 Orange Elephant	5	7.09 Go to Class	10
4.06 Bunny Hop	5	6.10 Just Like That	10	7.10 Don't Forget	5
4.07 Problem Detective	5	6.11 SDRAWKCAB	5	7.11 Column Relatives	10
4.08 Quadruple D	10	6.12 Wood You Believe?	10	7.12 Just Alike Only Different	10
4.09 Nitty Gritty	10	6.13 Fantasyland	10	7.13 It Came From Beneath the Blot	10
4.10 What Problem?	15	6.14 Silly Inventions	15	7.14 What's In a Name?	15
5.08 Goodness Sakes	15	6.15 Just Suppose	20	6.20 Paper Waltz	10
5.14 Goodness Sakes II	15			6.21 Strip Tease	10
				7.16 It Takes Two	15
				7.17 Alphabet Associations	15

carefully choose which exercises you use, because many require intense concentration.

2. Eliminate as many distractions as possible from your environment.
3. Maintain the progressive aspect of the exercises. Don't skip around.
4. If you don't complete an exercise within the prescribed period of time, leave it and go on to something else or to the next exercise. Then return to it and try again. If you still can't complete the exercise, wait until you have finished the phase you are in or until you have finished one run through of the program.
5. Try doing the program with one or more other people, either individually and then together or by starting as one, two or more groups. Carefully monitor the competitive spirit, however, so as not to create unnecessary obstacles. If you use competition, everyone should complete the program alone first, or at least the exercises you use during the competition.

EVALUATING AND MAINTAINING TRAINING PERFORMANCE

After completing the entire program, assess what you have learned and how you have changed since you began. Although self-evaluations (being objective about your own performance) are not easy, your program is not complete until you have evaluated your progress.

Begin evaluating your personal objectives by once again completing the Creative Problem-Solving Capability Rating Scale (Figure 3.1). Don't look at your original responses. Compare your two sets of responses to determine why you did or did not change in the direction you wanted. Determine in which specific areas you may need more practice. Finally, develop a plan to move yourself in the direction you want to go, even repeating the exercises that deal specifically with your problem areas.

Maintaining training performance involves conscious awareness of the correct thinking modes for different problems. Both logical/analytical/verbal thinking and holistic/intuitive/visual thinking are required to solve many problems. The particular mode used will depend on the stage of problem solving involved.

Become constantly aware of when to shift from one mode to the other through the use of refresher exercises. Twenty-eight exercises from this book that will help you develop such awareness are listed in Figure 3.5. Start with three to five exercises at a time and continue to use them as long as you feel the need. Try to do them rapidly and with as little effort as possible. Don't view the exercises as repetitive, but rather as new opportunities to grow creatively.

Figure 3.5 Refresher exercises.

4.01	6.13
4.02	6.14
4.03	
4.05	7.05
4.10	7.08
	7.11
5.01	7.12
5.02	
5.04	8.01
5.05	8.06
5.06	8.07
5.09	
5.10	9.02
	9.05
6.10	
6.11	10.01
	10.02
	10.03

4

Getting Ready

Before you begin a task, you need to obtain the necessary tools. Whether you plan to write a book, complete your taxes, paint a house, or go to war, you have to be prepared.

The task of creative problem solving is the same. Preparation is critical to solving most problems requiring creative approaches. And the most critical tool here is self-awareness.

But unlike house painting, no simple tools exist for scraping away the old paint that has collected on your mind, or for preparing the surface of your mind so that effective problem solving can begin.

You first need to analyze the surface of your mind and develop a greater awareness about your creativity potential. In which spots is the paint too thick? Where is it flaking off? Which spots would respond better to sandpaper and which to a scraping tool?

You must learn things about yourself that you can use to your best advantage in problem solving. And, you must get to know your problem.

Creative house painting.

Self-awareness and problem awareness are key ingredients for success in this endeavor. And both can be obtained through preparation. Once you develop self-awareness, most problems you encounter will be solved more easily. In contrast, problem awareness is a knowledge you will need every time you approach a new problem, for each new problem is a unique situation that presents different challenges.

The exercises in this chapter are designed to help you practice preparing for self- and problem-awareness. Some will help you to examine yourself and analyze how you solved past problems, consider your potential for creativity, and practice with ideas and visualizations. Other exercises are problem-oriented. They focus on speculation, processing information and creating new perspectives.

Not only can the exercises help you prepare for the exercises in the following chapters, but they will also prepare you to deal with daily problems you already encounter.

4.01 GOAL VISUALIZATION

It's easy to become blocked in problem solving when we consider the negative mental attitudes we developed when we failed before. But the proper mental attitude can increase the number of problems we're able to solve successfully.

Before beginning this exercise, assume that nothing is impossible and every problem, no matter how difficult, can be solved.

Write down a problem you successfully solved in the past.

____

____

____

____

How did you feel when you solved it (happy, relieved, excited)?

____________________ ____________________

____________________ ____________________

____________________ ____________________

Concentrate on these emotions. Did things turn out the way you had pictured them originally?

____

Why or why not?

____

____

____

____

Now imagine how things will be if you could solve a current problem. What will you be doing, how will you and others feel?

____

____

____

What will be better or worse?

____

____

____

____

What will be the same or different?

____

____

____

____

(While you're doing this, try to develop mental images for every detail of your solved problem.) You may also try imagining what the ideal solution would be like and how you would feel if you achieved it.

____

____

____

____

By concentrating on the emotions you experienced after successfully solving a problem, you will begin to develop success associations that will help you deal with subsequent problems.

Looking at the reasons you were able to solve the problem will contribute to the development of these success associations.

When you practiced concentrating on your current problem, did you imagine some of the same emotions you recalled from your earlier problem? If not, try to think of why you didn't make this association.

The most important aspect of this exercise is to develop the creative climate within yourself for creative problem solving. As the comic strip character Pogo said, "We have met the enemy and he is us." Avoid making yourself the major constraint in creative problem solving.

4.02 HOW MUCH ARE YOU WORTH?

It was once estimated that the chemical elements in the human body are worth about $1.98. That was, of course, before inflation; now we could probably purchase a Hawaiian condo in exchange for those chemicals.

We can't assign a dollar value to our human worth, but we can estimate its value in helping us achieve our creative potential. We will be crippled if we concentrate exclusively on our liabilities, and we will establish an almost insurmountable block of our creative potential.

How aware are you of your creative potential? List everything about yourself that you consider to be of positive worth.

____

____

Now, describe how these characteristics might help you enhance your creativity.

An example: If one of your positive features is punctuality, you might list reliability as something that indicates how you will be consistent in approaching problem solving.

4.03 THINK ABOUT IT

You're reading this book. That indicates you're interested in becoming more creative, whether generally or in a particular area.

However, concentrating on only one aspect of your life can be less desirable than trying to enhance your creativity in all your major life areas.

To start you thinking about this, make a list of all the things you could do to become more creative in different areas of your life.

In your job?

In your relationship(s) with your spouse or best friend?

With your children or others' children?

____

____

____

In your hobbies?

____

____

____

In your favorite sport or recreational activity?

____

____

____

To make this task easier, try listing the different types of activities or interactions involved in each area before you generate your creative alternatives.

The lists you developed will be unique to you and those with similar occupations and interests. What is important is to think of many different ways of doing things you do now. When you do things differently, you expand your awareness of how you use your creativity and how it can be enhanced.

4.04 EARLY BIRD

The extremely complex instrument known as the brain is capable of performing many activities, most of them consciously and some, below our conscious level.

Because there are so many different levels of brain activity, there is considerable variability in how we solve different problems. Ideas come to us at the strangest times – in the shower or while watching TV, driving, or reading.

We can capitalize on different intensities of brain-wave functioning. Depending on the time of day and our level of arousal, brain waves vary from very mild to very intense activity. During sleep, theta waves are projected from the brain; during times of busy thought, we produce beta waves.

Different types of brain waves are associated with different types of problem-solving activities. For instance, theta waves are ideal for divergent, non-judgmental thinking. When theta waves are present, analytical brain functions are repressed and it is easier for the brain to use free association and speculation.

By knowing when the brain is "holding" in different wave patterns, we can harness this information for our benefit. For example, when divergent thinking is needed, we can do it when theta waves are most likely to occur. Theta waves are most often present just before we fall asleep and just before or after we wake up.

The following simple exercise will help you harness your theta wave brain patterns. Apply it to one of your current problems.

1. Set your alarm clock to wake you up in the morning twenty to thirty minutes earlier than usual.
2. As soon as you can, sit down and begin free associating solutions to your problem.
3. Suspend all evaluation while you do this and continue writing down solutions until you have exhausted all possibilities.
4. Jot down how long you spent on this activity.
5. Do the same thing the next morning, but try to write for five minutes longer than you did the previous day. If you run out of ideas before the time limit is up, keep writing even if what you put down doesn't seem practical or make much sense.
6. Continue this exercise for at least a week. Then stop and see how much you have improved.

This exercise often generates initial solutions that are more logical and practical than later ones. Don't worry, however, because the ideas you produce later in the week frequently will result in the most creative solutions. Even if they at first appear illogical or impractical, you should be able to transform them into ideas with high potential for solving your problem.

4.05 IMAGINE THAT

Some successful problem-solvers have the ability to imagine themselves doing something and experiencing various sensations. Athletes do this, such as pole vaulters who picture themselves running toward the bar, planting the pole, lifting off and clearing the bar.

Imagination can help you deal with many problems. Use the following exercise to test your ability to develop images. Be as detailed as possible in your visualizations.

1. Think of yourself walking up some stairs.
2. Imagine the pain associated with a slight pin prick in your fingertip.
3. Feel a hot fire radiating off your back.
4. Visualize a rainy day in a forest.
5. Imagine the feeling of warmth when you first enter your house after being outside on a cold day.
6. Think of your bedroom when you were a child.
7. Imagine the sound of a jet airplane when it lands.
8. Picture yourself flying like a bird.
9. Imagine the texture and feel of a stucco wall.
10. Picture yourself riding a bicycle on a country road during the summer.
11. Picture yourself diving into a pool at the moment you first hit the water.
12. Think of the smell of raw onions.

To receive the maximum benefit from the exercise, concentrate very hard on each of the visualizations. A quick thought and image will not provide you with useful experience in visualization.

If you didn't visualize many details, try the exercise again when you can take your time and when you feel relaxed, perhaps after some deep-breathing exercises.

4.06 BUNNY HOP

The development of creative solutions often involves the ability to rearrange information to form new meanings. See if you can make your ideas multiply like a rabbit by forming as many words as possible, at least twelve, from the word RABBIT and from the word MULTIPLY.

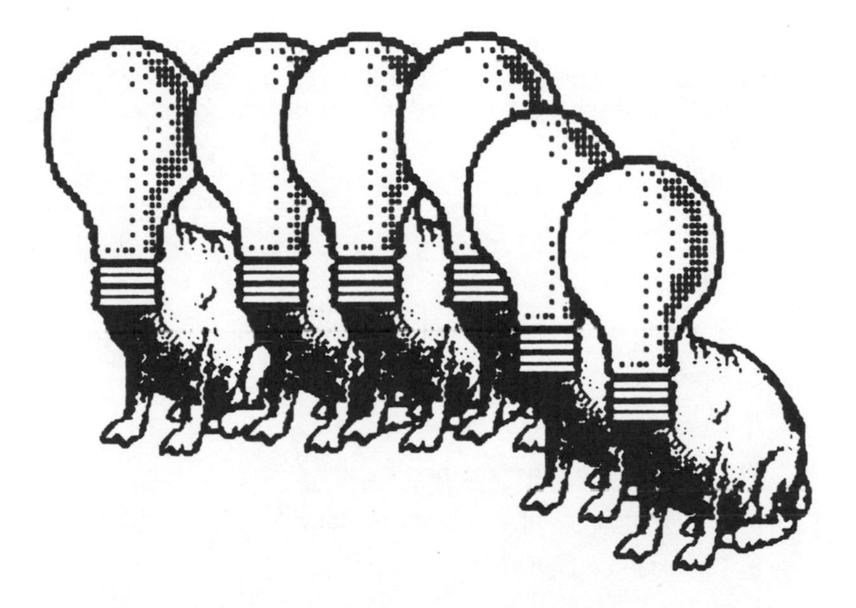

Ideas multiplying like rabbits.

4.07 PROBLEM DETECTIVE

When we first confront a problem, we often make snap judgments as to the cause of the problem. A creative solution, however, only can be achieved when we devote considerable time to analyzing the problem and generating a large number of possible explanations.

To become a "problem detective," be aware that most unstructured problems present few clues as to their solution. We must develop several hypotheses and later test them for their validity. The following statement is presented as a fact, but it may or may not be true. Develop as many different explanations as you can.

"Research has revealed that more people file for divorce during the summer than during any other season."

4.08 QUADRUPLE D

Sometimes creative problem-solving involves left-brain, or logical and analytical, types of thinking. This type is used to process information systematically.

Use this exercise to practice your skills in systematically processing information. From the information presented, determine who is the drunkard brother, assuming that being a drunkard is his occupation, and that each husband-and-wife pair lives together in the same city.

1. Four brothers lived in Detroit.
2. Dean married Dee Dee.
3. Dave moved to Denver.
4. The doctor brother moved to Duxbury.
5. Don married Darla.
6. Denise married the doctor brother.
7. The dentist brother married Danielle.
8. The druggist brother moved to Danville.
9. Dan married Denise.
10. Dee Dee lives in Dallas.

Unlike the other exercises in this book, there is a correct answer to this exercise. It is a very structured problem IF you know the correct procedure for solving it. (See page 60 for the answer AFTER you have tried solving the problem.)

4.09 NITTY GRITTY

Sometimes it is difficult to separate the relevant from the non-relevant in dealing with a problem, especially when we deal with familiar things. We must develop the ability to see things in terms of their usefulness so we won't be overwhelmed by the amount of information to be processed.

If you were to make improvements on the products listed on the next page, which attributes would you consider to be relevant and which less relevant?

1. Roller skates
2. Telephone
3. Calculator
4. Stapler
5. Light bulb
6. Typewriter
7. Bicycle
8. Door knob
9. Toaster
10. Clock

Relevance is a subjective matter depending on your objective for the items listed. The color of a telephone would be irrelevant if you intend to improve on the telephone's functioning, but relevant if you're concerned with appearance.

Think about why you categorized the attributes as relevant or non-relevant. Can you learn anything about yourself in terms of the value preferences you have for the objects, such as, do you value style over reliability, or both equally?

How many attributes did you list and how thorough were you? Could every attribute be used to make an improvement? Did you leave any out? If you visualized the product while you did this exercise, you probably didn't list as many attributes as you would have had you been looking directly at it. However, if you discover you omitted some attributes, it could be a comment on what you consciously or subconsciously consider to be important.

4.10 WHAT PROBLEM?

A frequent problem solving mistake is our tendency to plunge right in without considering the exact nature of the problem. We skim over any analysis of the situation and end up frustrated in our attempts to develop workable solutions.

The way we verbally define a problem is often too narrow or too broad in scope. This is an individual matter because the perceived scope will vary from person to person. In problem solving, you constantly should question if the problem is too broad or too narrow for *you* to tackle.

One method to achieve the proper scope is to ask Who? What? Where? When? Why? about the initial statement. Answer each question in as many ways as possible and select from the answers as many elements as you would like to include in your refined problem statement.

Example: In what ways might people be motivated?

Questions	Possible Answers . . . .
WHO should be motivated?	Workers, students
WHAT kind of motivation?	To achieve performance objectives, do homework
WHERE is the motivation?	Within people; external to people; groups
WHEN are peole motivated?	When needs are likely to be satisfied
WHY motivate people?	To get something accomplished, to satisfy needs.

From these possible answers, the following refined problem statements could be formulated:

1. In what ways might students motivate themselves to do homework?
2. In what ways might we satisfy worker needs?
3. In what ways might we reward workers for satisfying their own and organizational needs?

These statements provide a focus different from the original broad statement. Also note that there are no correct questions or answers; your only objective is to create a new problem perspective.

Here's another example:

In what ways might I better dry my hair?

Questions	Possible Answers . . . .
WHO needs hair dried?	People, people who get caught in the rain.
WHAT kind of hair?	Human
WHERE is the hair?	On the head
WHEN is the hair dried?	After it gets wet, when moisture is removed.
WHY dry hair?	So it won't be wet, to avoid catching cold.

Possible restatements:

1. In what ways might human head hair be dried?
2. In what ways might moisture be removed from hair?
3. In what ways might I lessen the chances of catching cold?

Your turn!

In what ways might interpersonal conflict be reduced?

Questions	Possible Answers ....
WHO has conflict?	
WHAT kind of conflict?	
WHERE is the conflict?	
WHEN is the conflict?	
WHY is there conflict?	
OR	
WHY reduce conflict?	

In what ways might cutting grass be improved?

Questions	Possible Answers ....
WHO has grass?	
WHAT kind of grass?	
WHERE is the grass?	
WHEN does the grass need cutting?	
WHY cut the grass?	

4.11 GOOD SENSE SHOPPING

At Christmas time, many of us make repeated trips to the store when we forget to buy something. We have to face the crowds and traffic, and remember where the store displays the item.

When we try to remember a location, we use visual imagery.

In the case of the store, you use a cognitive map by relating objects to other objects and reference points. For instance, suppose you want to buy a leadership book but you can't remember where the store is located.

To construct a cognitive map, you would visualize the bookstore and remember it is located in a mall near a large bank. Once inside the mall, you would visualize the store and recall it is near a men's clothing store. Inside the bookstore, you visualize the book's location as near the business books which are just past the history section. You remember that the book is on a lower shelf next to some red books.

The following visualization exercise provides an in-depth sensory experience, because you focus intensively on each scene.

Think of a store where you shop frequently. Visualize general areas first, such as shape, size and the location of different departments. Next focus upon one specific department, such as jewelry. Concentrate all your imagery powers upon this location. Visualize everything that exists, including sales personnel, customers, types of jewelry, display cases, sounds, smells and textures. If you have shopped at this store for at least a year, you can also try this exercise using the four seasons. Is there a difference in how things look in the winter as opposed to the summer? What accounts for this difference?

4.12 VISUAL SMORGASBORD

It is difficult to visualize things which are unfamiliar. However, that is just what we must do to develop creative solutions. We must imagine in our mind's eye elements of the unknown and then view them in detail and in relation to other elements. The better we can do this, the more freely problem solutions will flow.

An added benefit of this exercise is that it helps stimulate originality, because you are forced to create your responses with ambiguous initial perceptions. As you elaborate upon your visions, the perceptions gradually become more familiar. The result is an original product.

Visualize the following things in as much detail as possible.

1. A dog with nine legs

2. A fly twelve feet high

3. A robot anteater
4. Asparagus rockets
5. A chocolate egg pounding on a diamond nail with a macaroni hammer

4.13 MIND MAPS

We use associations to think, one thought prompting a second which prompts a third and so on. As we associate, concepts form, and we then use these concepts to solve a problem.

To record creative thought processes, we should use creative recording methods as opposed to sequential methods, such as outlines.

Tony Buzan's book *Brain Mapping* presents a relatively simple way to organize information and stimulate creative thinking. In contrast to outlines, which require linear thinking, brain maps allow us to list ideas as we think of them. We can associate from one idea to another. Brain maps allow us to think the way our minds work.

A brain map is illustrated in Figure 4.1 on the next page. The problem involves setting up a new house. Begin with a central concept. In this case, draw a circle in the center of a paper for the word "house." Next, draw a line to a circle representing some aspect of the problem. Note in the example how one of the lines goes to furniture. At this point, you might think of money and draw a circle representing finances. Then you might revert to furniture and begin listing examples: sofa, recliner, TV, bed. The bed, in turn, might stimulate thinking about sheets, blankets and a comforter.

Now you try it. Develop a brain map using creativity as the central concept. As you continue to generate ideas, write down whatever pops into your head. Your map will differ from other people's, because each map reflects unique thinking processes.

4.14 NAME THAT LETTER

Our ability to analyze a problem often determines our ability to solve it. Analysis involves creative thought, because data must be generated and combined in unique ways to comprehend a situation. This exercise requires you to stretch your imagination while analyzing the problem.

Figure 4.1 Example of brain mapping.

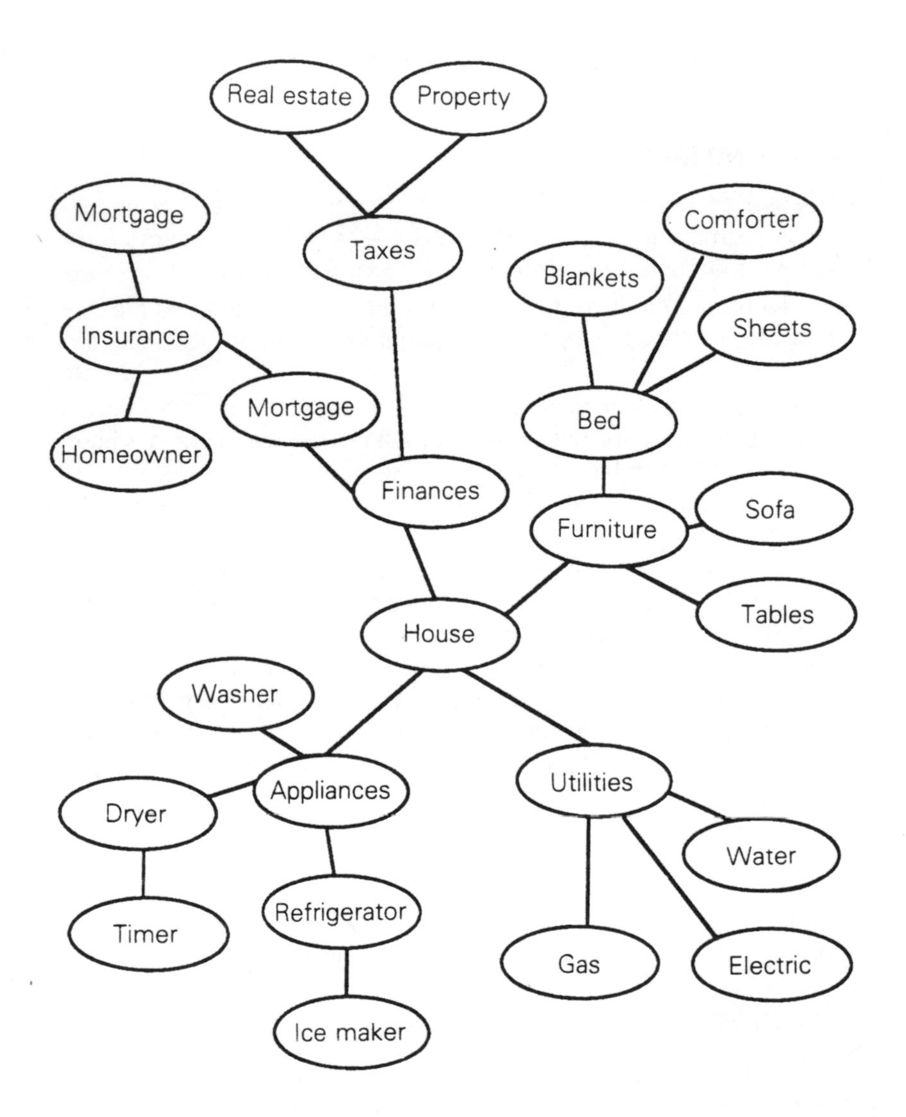

What is the next letter in this sequence? O T T F F S S

The "logical" solution, which is the answer given by whomever developed the puzzle, is the letter "E." Each of the other letters represents the first letter in the numbers "one" through "seven." However, you may have thought of another "logical" solution, the letter "L" for example.

Assume that each letter of the alphabet is assigned a consecutive number value between one and twenty-six. "A" would be one, "B" would be two, "Z" would be twenty-six. That would make the sequence of numbers 15, 20, 20, 6, 6, 19, 19. The numerical difference between each of these numbers is 5, 0, 14, 0, 13, and 10. That is, fifteen minus 20 is 5, 20 minus 20 is 0, etc. With the exception of the five, the pattern shows that descending numbers are preceded and followed by zeros. Thus the next number in the series should be twelve, and the letter corresponding to twelve is "L."

4.15 DISFIGURED

Which figure does not belong here?

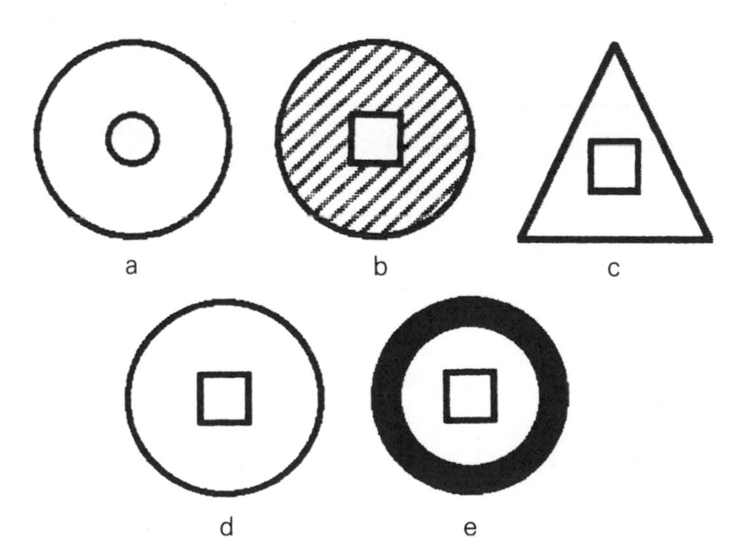

The correct answer is, of course, "c," because its outer shape is a triangle while the others are circles. Yeah, that's it. But wait . . .

hmmmmmm. It could be "a" because that's the only one with a circle at its center and not a square. Okay, I'm positive now. Then again . . . the answer may be "e" because it has a thicker outer line than the others. But "b" has stripes . . . And so on.

There obviously is no "correct" solution. Correctness in this case depends upon your viewpoint. Any one of the figures might not belong and you could be correct.

The point illustrated here is we must know what type of problem we face. Is it open-ended, requiring divergent, creative thinking? If there had been only one correct response, analytical thinking would have been more appropriate.

SOLUTION TO 4.08 QUADRUPLED

All that is required to solve this problem is constructing a simple matrix using each of the four 'D' categories, plugging in the information as it becomes available, and returning to previous information to fill in the gaps. The "correct" answer is Dean.

What's Happening

The ten exercises in this chapter will help you develop self- and problem-awareness. They are designed to heighten specific sensory areas: observation, hearing, visualizing, seeing, tasting, touching, smelling and empathy. Some exercises also will deal with developing a positive mental attitude, concentration and imagery.

The exercises should give you an increased ability to experience your environment with all of your senses. For example, something as simple as an ashtray can be experienced in more ways than you might consider. Obviously you can see and touch it, but how often have you used your other senses to describe the ashtray? Have you ever tasted it? Somewhat repulsive, certainly, but we do need to use all of our senses to become better problem solvers.

In addition to breeding contempt, familiarity dulls our senses. Most of us become so immune to our daily environments that we rarely notice anything new or different. The same holds true for the problems we face. Sometimes we fail to solve a problem because we viewed it as similar to another problem, when it actually may have been a variation on the same TYPE of problem.

These exercises will help you realize that there is a whole new world out there waiting to be experienced. You just have to know what's happening.

5.01 YOUR ROOM

For this exercise, find a comfortable chair in a room of your choice. The room you are in right now is "your room," because, although it may not actually belong to you, it is yours in at least sensory ownership. Begin to think of it as YOURS and no one else's; what happens here is in your control.

Begin by describing the room. How large is it? Are you alone here? If not, who are the other people and what are they doing? How many walls are there and what colors are they? Are they panelled or papered? How are the ceiling and floors different from the walls? What objects are in your room? How are they arranged? Why are they here?

Continue to visually explore your room for about five minutes, describing everything you can see. Then change your position and see if there is anything you missed. Can you see shadows now that you didn't see before? How might the colors here change during different times of day? Not including objects, try to describe your room in at least thirty different ways.

Now, go to another room and do the exercise again, this time allowing yourself only two minutes to describe as many features as you can.

If you had any trouble noticing or describing everything in your room, you are probably afflicted with the disease known as familiarity, a fixed way of thinking and seeing.

Try to rev up your right brain a little each day by noticing something in your everyday environment. Maybe it will be something as simple as noticing the texture of the roof on the house across the street. It doesn't matter what you notice or how you do it. You need to awaken those stimuli that died so long ago. If you do this regularly, you will do something positive to make your right brain a little more alive every day.

5.02 THE PICNIC

For this exercise put yourself into a relatively relaxed state of mind. Let your thoughts flow easily and experience vicariously many different sensations.

Imagine you are on a picnic in a secluded area far away from the city. Our picnic site is an open, grassy area surrounded by trees, with a small stream nearby. You have brought a picnic basket and a blanket. You are there with a special friend and three children who are playing about thirty yards from you.

Begin by concentrating on this scene. Then try to gradually add more detail. What do the children look like? How are they dressed? What colors are they wearing? What are they playing? Where is the stream from where you are now sitting or standing? What does your picnic basket look like? How far away are the trees? Continue to add detail in this manner for another two or three minutes.

Now try to experience the many different textures present.

What does the grass feel like? The blanket? The picnic basket? Can you imagine the textural contrasts of the different types of tree bark? Are there any rocks in the stream? If so, how do they differ in texture? Stick your bare feet in the stream. How does it feel?

Concentrate next on smells. What do the grass and the food in the picnic basket smell like? Does the blanket have a particular odor? Perhaps a horse just galloped through your picnic area and left its own special smell.

After you have thought of and attempted to experience all the smells present, direct your attention to sounds. What do you hear? Listen very carefully. Can you hear yourself talking and the children playing at the same time? How does the stream sound? Think of the wind blowing through the trees, and imagine the different sounds produced as the wind speed varies. Take an apple from your picnic basket and bite into it. What sound does it make? Think of other foods you might have in your basket and how they sound when you bite into them.

To benefit most from this exercise, concentrate fully and attempt to introduce as much detail as possible. The ability to perform this exercise is critical to development of sensory awareness about all types of problems. Without this awareness, we can overlook characteristics vital to achieving a creative solution.

If you had trouble with the exercise, you may have rushed through it too quickly. If so, try it again, allowing sufficient time for all appropriate connections to be made within your brain.

5.03 TOUCH IT

The sense of touch may be one of our less frequently used senses. We often take it for granted since we typically use some of our other senses more frequently. As a consequence, touching sensations may not be as well-developed as seeing, due to limited sensory experiences in touching. Most blind people exhibit greater facility in this sense than we who are "handicapped" by our seeing abilities.

In this exercise, try to shut out all your senses except touch. Ignore smells, sights, sounds, and tastes. Concentrate only on the sensations transmitted by your fingertips.

Place the following objects (or similar ones) in a medium-sized box or sack: a penny, a dime, a cotton ball, a pen or pencil, a small ball, a stick of gum, a key, a die or sugar cube, a small paper wad, and a square of sandpaper or an emery board. Without looking at

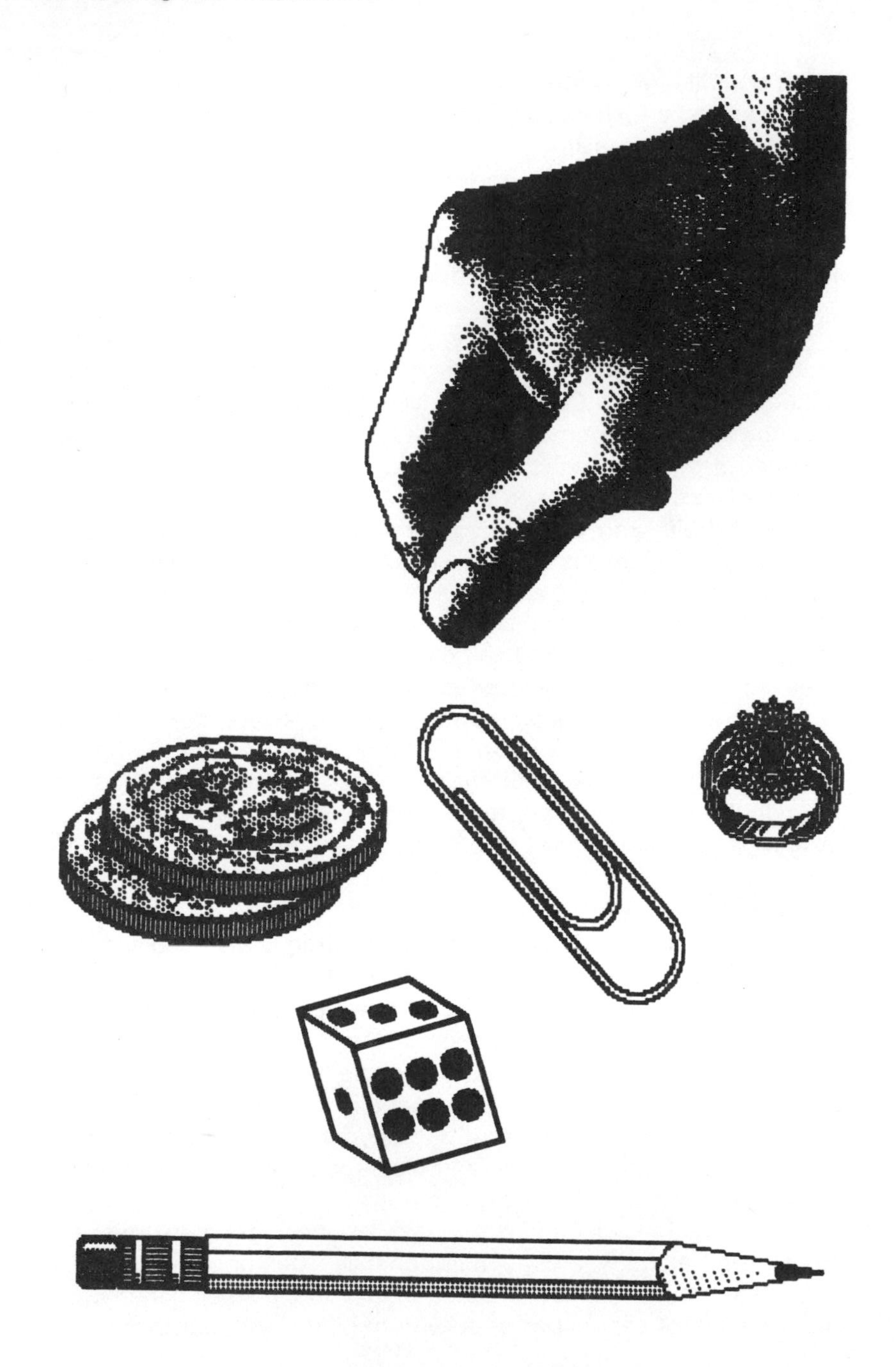

any of the objects, reach in and identify each one by touch. Withdrawing your hand, visualize each object in as much detail as possible. Now reach into the box or bag again and examine each object by touch to see if you left out any features you had visualized. For example, did you remember to visualize the raised portions on the coins and the rough edges on the dime? Did you have any trouble distinguishing the dime from the penny? Did the ball seem smaller or larger than you had imagined? Finally, select two objects at random (without looking) and compare them in as many ways as you can, using only your sense of touch. You should have had little difficulty identifying the objects by touch, except possibly for the penny and the dime. You were forced to rely exclusively on touch to make the distinction.

Visualizing objects and then identifying them by touch can produce surprising results. Even when we are familiar with objects by both sight and touch, seeing will dominate due to its ability to provide more information. If you decide to use your pen, you need only to look at it, recognize it and put it to use. The same thing can be done using touch, but it will take longer. You first must recognize the pen by its shape and texture and then determine which end the cap is on.

If you didn't experience similar differences with the other objects, repeat the exercise, concentrating more on the differences between touch and sight.

5.04 I HEAR YA

Hearing is another sense we frequently take for granted. Although we are exposed to a variety of sounds daily, we rarely hear them all. We are usually too busy thinking or attending to our other senses to hear everything going on around us. And with good reason, too. If we turned on all our senses to their full capacity at the same time, we would be overwhelmed by the amount of data our brains would have to process.

For this exercise, first imagine the following sounds:

- the engine of a car or truck
- wind blowing
- bird calls
- screeching tires
- car horns
- someone walking
- hands brushing clothing
- people talking
- dogs barking
- sirens
- your own breathing
- music

Then take a walk on a relatively busy street and try to hear each one of these sounds, or any different ones. Really concentrate, since what you are trying to do is *experience* the sounds and not just notice them.

How successful were you in hearing the sounds? Could you EXPERIENCE them as separate sounds of environmental stimuli? Can you easily distinguish between two or more sounds that occur at the same time?

Pay particular attention to the various characteristics of the different sounds. Can you detect variances in pitch, timbre and amplitude? Are you able to sense the upper ranges of sounds such as bird calls and screeching tires? How are they different? Continue to examine these sounds in as many ways as you can, until you have begun to master sound.

5.05 SENSORY STRETCH

Although we are well equipped to experience our environment, the sensory mechanisms we use often deceive us. For example, if a person you know to be six feet tall stands a quarter of a mile from you, he or she will appear to be much shorter to the unaided eye. Obviously, the person's height doesn't change. What does change is our perception of the situation. In a similar manner, heat radiating from a highway on a hot day will look like water when viewed from a distance. Again, our perceptions are distorted by our sensory mechanisms.

When you think about it, we are constantly being misled by our senses. We need to become more aware of the limits of our senses. One way to do this is to exaggerate or stretch the functions normally performed by each of the five senses.

As a test of how in tune you are with your senses, answer the questions that follow. For each answer, try to think of why you responded the way you did.

1. What color is happiness?
2. What color is Monday?
3. What does blue smell like?
4. How would you describe the texture of yellow?
5. What does a peach sound like?

6. What does red taste like?
7. How would your eyes feel if they could "touch" sandpaper by only looking at it?
8. What does a ray of sun smell like?
9. What does a rose look like to another rose?
10. What color is the ticking of a clock?

While there can be no right or wrong answers here, what you should gain is a feeling for how easily you can distort your sensory mechanisms and apply them to other functions.

The reasons you gave for your answers can be a clue to your experiential background. If you described Monday as blue, you may

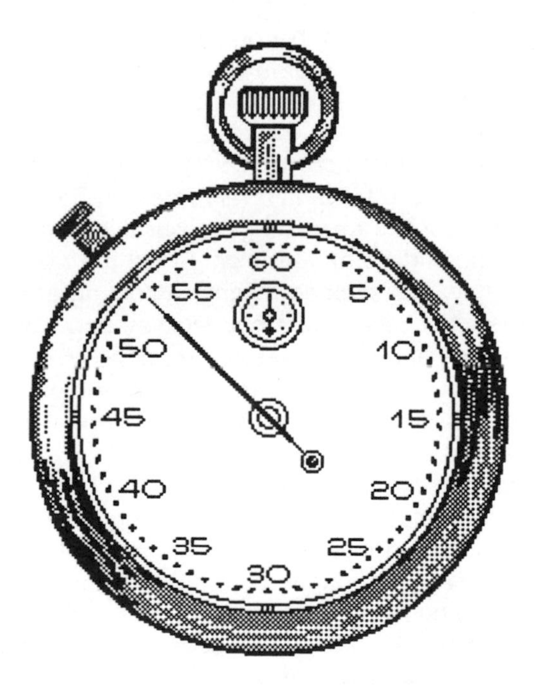

Color me timely.

feel depressed every Monday, or you may associate it with the notion of "blue Mondays." If you described yellow as feeling smooth, you may be relating it to butter.

If you had trouble distorting any of your senses, it may stem from deficiencies in your sensory background. For instance, I have heard people say they find it hard to hear things unless they wear their glasses. This dramatizes how heightened sensory awareness can develop creativity.

5.06 BE A BANANA

The ability to empathize with living and nonliving things is a critical skill required of all creative thinkers. Empathy creates awareness that leads to understanding. Understanding is essential for dealing with most kinds of problems. Without it, we only can bring limited resources to our problems. Creative solutions to some difficult problems can be achieved only by becoming deeply involved with the problem. We should try to become a problem whenever possible, to reveal new insights that could not be obtained from just being on the outside looking in.

Using all the concentration you can, try this exercise:

You are a banana. You live in a rain forest in South America. It is raining, and tiny droplets are running off your skin. Feel the droplets. Let them soak the surface of your skin. Smell the rain. What does it smell like? It now has stopped raining. A cool breeze is blowing, and you and the other bananas are bouncing around, swaying in the wind. Feel the wind and experience the motions. What sensations are there as your skin rubs against the skins of the other bananas? Look down and see the ground as you sway back and forth. Look up and see the tops of the trees. Now the wind is dying down. The oppressive heat is returning. Feel the warmth of the sun on your skin. Let the last bit of moisture on your skin dry up and evaporate. Suddenly there is tension in the air. Hear the birds in the trees around you call out their warning sounds. Feel the pressure on your tree. You are now swaying in jerky movements, but there is no breeze. The movements stop. An intense pressure grips you and squeezes ever tighter. Feel this pressure as you are being squeezed inward. Now you are being torn away from the other bananas by a large hairy hand. Feel the hand's texture on your skin. Hear the sound made as your stem is cracked and twisted. You are now separated and without the contact of the other banana skins. But the intense pressure continues. A sharp pain develops in the end of you. A small cut is made in one of the seams of your skin. Feel this pain and experience the small amount of air that enters the cut. Now your skin is being ripped down your side in large strips . . . one, two, three, four strips. Your insides are now exposed and shocked as they try to adjust to the sudden lack of warmth and darkness. Feel the sun and air on your fruit. What does it smell like? You are now completely free of your skin. Hot animal breath is enveloping you and it is becoming dark. Sharp incisors cut into your upper half, tearing it away from the lower. Imagine the fibers being torn away as your fruit is mixed with saliva. Feel the juice from your fruit and the saliva mixing together. Now your bottom half is gone. Don't you wish you were an animal?

Contemplating yellow things.

To benefit from this exercise, intensely focus your senses on achieving a maximum level of sensory arousal. You will find it is much easier to do the exercise if you have someone read it to you while you close your eyes, relax and try to concentrate.

5.07 MOWING ALONG

Write down three to five comments about the proposed design for a lawn mower shown in Figure 5.1. Did you make these or similar comments?

1. It is too high off the ground.
2. One of the wheels is too big (or too small).
3. It has two handles, where only one is needed.
4. The handles are too short.

Figure 5.1 Proposed design for a lawn mower.

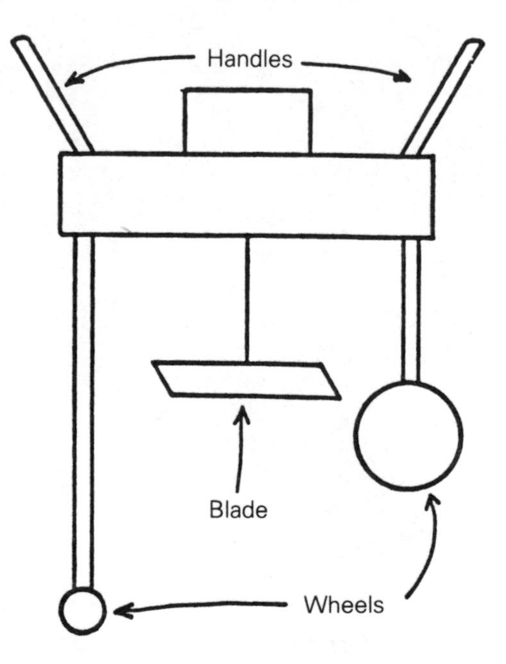

All of these comments are negative ones. Although criticism is not entirely undesirable, too much may stifle creativity. Most of us unfortunately have been conditioned to respond in an almost entirely negative manner.

Try the exercise again, only this time notice some positive aspects. For instance, would the size difference in the wheels make the mower ideal for steep hills?

5.08 GOODNESS SAKES

Many potentially useful ideas are lost because of our inability to suspend judgment and look for the positive aspects of new ideas. While not all ideas are initially proposed in a workable form, a few changes often can lead to a more feasible idea. In addition, what frequently appears to be a silly idea to one person may be used by another as a stimulus for more practical solutions. There is really no such thing as a silly idea, since all ideas have hidden within them the potential to produce solutions. It simply takes a little digging around to find these solutions.

See if you can think of at least three positive aspects for each of the following proposed products. If you can't think of anything positive, try to develop some modifications that might make the idea workable.

1. A square pencil
2. A glass mailbox
3. A wooden automobile tire
4. A house made of oatmeal
5. A ceiling clock
6. A foam-rubber airplane
7. A drinking glass that dissolves in water
8. Cement underwear
9. Neon eyeglasses

To get started, you might imagine that a square pencil won't roll off tables, a glass mailbox makes it easy to see if you have any mail, and a wooden automobile tire could be burned when it is worn out.

5.09 CUBE IMAGERY

One important function served by the right brain is manipulation of spatial relationships. The ability to recall and visualize images occurring in space is as essential to creative thinking as is the ability to recall and use words. Unfortunately, not all people exercise their visualization skills as much as they could; consequently, they believe they are not very good at visualization. With a little practice and concentration, however, all of us can improve.

Repeat this exercise several times until you can do it easily.

First, visualize a row of three cubes in front of you. The cube in the center is yellow and those on the ends are green. Now imagine that you move the yellow cube to the right end of the row and the cube on the right end to the center. What is the order of colors?

Easy? OK, then imagine that you move the cube now in the center to the left end and the cube that was on the left end to the right end. Now what does the row of colors look like?

No challenge? Well, make it more difficult by starting over again with two rows, the first with three green cubes and the second with three yellow cubes. Take the green cube on the left end and exchange it with the yellow cube in the middle. Then take the yellow cube on the right end of the second row and exchange it with the green cube in the middle of the first row. Finally, take the cube on the left end of the first row and exchange it with the cube in the middle of the second row. What is the order of colors in the two rows?

If you were easily able to visualize the two rows of cubes, you already have good visualization skills. Perhaps you, as would most people, memorized the sequence of colors after each operation and then made the necessary adjustments.

If you had trouble seeing the different moves, try reading one of the moves and then shut your eyes, fixing it in your memory. Concentrate on the pattern until it becomes locked in. Do this with each move until you can see the final pattern of colors.

Don't try to hurry through the exercise. Most of us are unaccustomed to mental manipulations like this, and time is required to practice the different stages involved.

5.10 ORANGE ELEPHANT

Get ready to time yourself. Do you have a watch or a clock with a second hand? Good. Now, for the next fifteen seconds, concentrate real hard on *not* thinking of an orange elephant. OK, time's up. Now tell the truth. Didn't you think of that elephant at least once during the fifteen seconds? It's not so easy, is it?

A simple act of concentration can be very difficult, depending on your state of mind, the external environment, and the amount of practice you've had in really concentrating on something. Yet, concentration is essential for creativity or any type of activity that requires focused effort.

We all differ in our ability to concentrate. Just think of the study habits you and your friends had while in school. Some people seem capable of intense study even under the most adverse conditions, including the sounds of blaring radios and TVs. Other people, in contrast, tend to be disturbed by the slightest sound.

One thing is fairly certain, however. Our concentration skills can be improved with practice. To improve your skills in this area, try this exercise.

Multiply 3 x 2 in your imagination. As you do it, think of each number and the final product. Do the same thing with 30 x 2, 30 x 3, and 40 x 6. Now multiply the following numbers and try to concentrate as hard as possible on all of the operations involved:

130 x 2	24 x 2	125 x 2
130 x 3	24 x 3	135 x 3
130 x 4	24 x 4	145 x 4

If you had trouble performing the calculations, think of that orange elephant. First, fix the numbers in your mind. Each time you come up with a digit in the total, think "orange elephant." For example, to multiply 125 by 2, think in this fashion: 5 x 2 equals 10, ZERO orange elephant; 2 x 2 equals four plus 1 is FIVE orange elephants; 2 x 1 equals TWO orange elephants. Put together the orange elephants in reverse order and you get 250.

If you had trouble fixing the numbers in your imagination, you also can use the orange elephant to help. Think of each number as a large numeral in a vivid orange color. If this doesn't work for you, assign a different color, such as blue to the number in the second row. Example: 145 orange elephants times 3 blue orange elephants.

Keep practicing until you easily can do all of the operations. If you would like a slightly different challenge, try using division problems.

5.11 BRAIN VACATION

Think of the last vacation you took. Visualize it in detail and recall everything you saw and did. What sensory experiences stand out? Why did you remember these experiences over others?

If it hasn't been too long since you took a vacation, it should have been easy for you to recall. And, if you had pleasant experiences, your memory probably worked well for you. I still can recall sensory experiences from a European vacation I took almost fifteen years ago, the smell of musty stone buildings in England and the taste of a yellow Italian wine.

Can you remember colors from your vacation? How vivid are they? What about textures? Do any stand out in your memory? In addition to how pleasant your experiences were, you probably recalled some things because of a sensory preference. Researchers think some of us are visual thinkers, while others rely more upon other senses. If most of your recollections were visual, you may be a visual thinker. Or, did you recall mostly smells? Do you "see" what I am saying?

5.12 THOUGHTFUL IMAGES

What images appear when you think of the following words: truth, solitude, quiet, anger, rough?

Similar to other visualization exercises, this one differs in one important way. Instead of visualizing tangible objects, you must think of abstract concepts. This is more difficult, since there are no concrete reference points. In contrast, it is easy to conjure up an image of something such as a lamp. It has clearly definable characteristics. Your choices are limited to deciding upon what type of lamp to visualize. What you visualized in this exercise also may be significant. Why did you think of the images you did? Do they possess emotional significance? Or, have you used an image before and simply recalled it from memory? For instance, you always might think of a particular section of a brick wall whenever you see or hear the word "rough."

5.13 WORKING OUT

In his excellent book, *Pumping Ions,* Tom Wujec describes the following visualization exercise. First, think of something you do at work which you dislike or find uncomfortable. Concentrate upon visualizing yourself doing this activity poorly. Then, picture yourself doing it well.

In what ways did your performance improve when you visualized yourself doing well? What emotions did you experience from this exercise? How did your emotions differ with the two parts of this exercise? You probably experienced some frustration when performing poorly and satisfaction when performing well.

When you evaluate your reactions to this exercise, consider how they differ from similar exercises. A distinctive feature of this exercise is that you visualized the same scene two different ways. The reason you experienced different emotional reactions was because of the change in visual content. Changing the content elicited different emotions which, in turn, affected your overall reaction to the exercise.

5.14 GOODNESS SAKES II

In Exercise 5.08, "Goodness Sakes," you were asked to think of positive things about some rather odd ideas. For instance, you were asked to list good things about a square pencil, a glass mailbox, and a wooden automobile tire. Although this is a useful sensory stretch exercise, the content is not realistic. You also can benefit from true-to-life situations. For this exercise, list positive things about the following:

1. Having surgery in the hospital.
2. Being fired from your job.
3. Losing all your money.

The situations in this version of Goodness Sakes require you to think more seriously about your responses. As a result, you may have more trouble thinking of positive aspects. Some possible responses follow.

1. Being in the hospital for surgery:
   You may get better.
   You will get a vacation from work.
   You will learn how a hospital functions.
   If you like drugs, you will receive some pain killers.
   You will receive a lot of sympathy.
   You may receive free flowers and other gifts.

2. Getting fired from your job:
   You will have the opportunity to start your own business.
   You will meet new people while job hunting.
   You no longer will have to tolerate obnoxious co-workers.
   You finally can "tell off" that overbearing boss.
   You may get to travel more than ever while job hunting.
   You may learn first hand about how the welfare system works.

3. Losing all of your money:
   You will learn first hand about how the welfare system works.
   You finally can "tell off" the IRS (if you plan to stay penniless).
   You will decrease the odds of getting germs from dirty money.
   That bothersome rattle of change in your pocket will disappear.
   People no longer will ask to borrow money from you.
   Men can eliminate that annoying wallet lump in their pockets.
   You have the perfect opportunity to sharpen your begging skills.
   Your creative thinking abilities will be tested to the limit.

5.15 SQUARE SEARCH

Look around the room you are now in and find five things which contain squares or rectangles. Then, try to find five more. Continue to do this until you have found every possible square or rectangle in the room.

For many years I have noticed that whenever I buy a new car, I am more likely to notice others driving the same car. This is because I am using what psychologists refer to as "selective attention." That is, I consciously pay attention to certain things in my environment.

When you deal with a problem, you also use selective attention. You pay attention to those problem features you have experienced and seen. And, when you concentrate upon a particular feature, this is where you will search for solutions. Sometimes, this works well and you solve the problem; other times, it does not work, and you are stymied.

If you become blocked during problem solving, remember selective attention. Chances are this is what is giving you trouble. To avoid selective attention, concentrate upon another feature of the problem. For instance, table lamp designers might experience trouble thinking of new designs. However, if they would shift their attention from the physical features to *how* a lamp is used, new ideas might emerge.

5.16 TABLOID ATTENTION

Do you read a newspaper or a magazine regularly? What specific articles or features do you pay attention to? Why do you focus upon these and not others?

This is another exercise on selection attention. We pay attention to our needs, what we can relate to, and what we most recently have noticed. This particular exercise will help you learn more about your needs and values. The newspaper and magazine articles you attend to are determined, in part, by your values. And, these values often are relative rather than absolute. For instance, you may be interested in articles on both finances and recreation. However, you are likely to focus upon financial articles if your value preferences are stronger in this area.

Creative problem solving also requires selective attention. When you solve problems creatively, you use values to guide your choices. For instance, you must decide what data to use for problem analysis and which ideas are most likely to resolve your problems. Thus, selective attention can be a positive force. It also can be negative. Your values sometimes will bias you in a nonproductive way. If you need to make a financial decision, for example, you may look for a low-yield, short-term gain. However, it may be better to assume a high-yield, long-term gain.

5.17 PLANE TO SEE

Visualize the inside of an airplane. Try to see all details and things you typically might not notice while flying. Look at specific colors, shapes, textures, and different objects and people. Now, imagine that the airplane is flying and so are you. That is, see yourself flying about inside the cabin while in flight. Zoom up and down the aisle. Oops! You almost hit a flight attendant. Be more careful. Fly down the aisle and hover above a row of seats. What do the people look like? What are they doing? Now, get small. Visualize that you are so small you can fly about without being seen. Explore the entire cabin. Zip around the serving cart and notice everything on it. Fly under and beside the seats. Visit an overhead baggage compartment.

Peek inside someone's briefcase. Finally, get even smaller and faster. Zoom between microscopic cracks in the floor and visit the baggage area. Bark at an obnoxious, barking dog. Travel through a tiny crack to the outside of the aircraft and examine the metal skin. Fly around to the windshield and wave to the cockpit crew. Tell them you didn't like the meal and what they can do about it. Don't worry. They can't see you.

Unlike other visualization exercises, this one uses progressive instructions. That is, I asked you to imagine yourself becoming smaller and smaller and seeing increasing amounts of detail. This process of gradually increasing visual detail can enhance the vividness of images. As with most mental or physical activities, performance can be increased if movement toward a goal is incremental.

I recently noticed the importance of image vividness during a visit to the National Gallery in Washington, D.C. While walking through the impressionism section, I observed several artists making copies of famous paintings by Renoir, Manet, and others. Most of these artists were very good. They certainly possessed more artistic skill than most of us ever will have. And their copies were excellent. However, their renditions of the masterpieces lacked one major ingredient: vividness. In all the copies I saw, each one lacked a sharpness of detail present in the original.

I am not an artist and I have no formal artistic training. So, I only can speculate from a layman's viewpoint as to why the copies lacked vividness. It is possible that the artists may have transferred the original images too directly. That is, they were working quickly and not taking the time to experience the scenes in as much progressive detail as the original artists.

The same thing can happen if you try to visualize a problem solution too quickly. Take your time and imagine the problem and possible solutions in detail. However, gradually add more detail as you think of it. Most good solutions result from a cumulative process and should not be hurried.

6

Loosening Up Your Mind

Left-brain analytical problem-solving involves the logical and systematic application of old ways of looking at problems. Once problems are diagnosed and a known solution reached, the outcome will be either correct or incorrect.

In contrast, right-brain problem solving develops new ways of approaching problems without regard to a logical procedure. The end result cannot be classified as either right or wrong, because any approach may produce a creative outcome.

The exercises in this chapter deal with specific flexibility areas such as breaking away from constraints, testing assumptions and problem boundaries, categorizing and redefining symbols, breaking problems down and analyzing them, analogies, reversals, distortions, fantasy and hypothetical situations. In short, the exercises will help you loosen up your mind.

6.01 SQUARE OFF

This classic example stresses the importance of not making unwarranted assumptions based on our initial perceptions. How many squares are there in Figure 6.1 below?

Figure 6.1

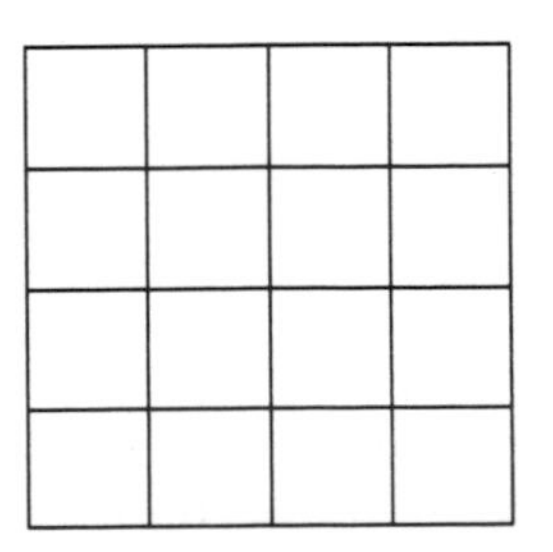

If you are like many people, your initial response was sixteen, or perhaps seventeen squares if you included the border. You would have been making an incorrect assumption about the problem, probably because of the constraints of viewing a square as a unitary figure.

At least thirty-five squares can be found using the sixteen smaller squares, different positions of two-by-two and three-by-three squares and by using the small squares as borders for other squares. More creative viewpoints might yield even more squares. An assumption might also have been made that the squares are located in unidimensional space (a flat plane). What if the problem was considered as existing in multidimensional space? The number of squares would be infinite, bound only by your views on the size and form of the universe.

Have you ever placed similar constraints on yourself when you tried to solve a problem? If we are to overcome such constraints, we must test continually all assumptions we make.

6.02 DON'T FENCE ME IN

We frequently place a constraint on ourselves by making unwarranted assumptions about a problem's boundaries, typically reflected in our initial statement of the problem. For example, increasing available parking spaces on an overcrowded campus contains the assumption that cars (as opposed to buses or subways) are the only means of transportation available. Or that the only parking available is on-campus.

To help break away from such a constraining tendency, identify the assumptions made in the following statements:

1. To design a battery-powered calculator capable of performing all the operations needed by an accountant.
2. To build a better garbage can.
3. To design a better door lock for the home in order to reduce burglaries.
4. To design a telephone cord that won't tangle and makes it easy to use the receiver from a distance of at least fifty feet.
5. To design scissors that are less fatiguing to use.

To help you redefine the problem boundaries and to avoid making unwarranted assumptions about each statement, here are some questions to get you started.

1. Why a calculator? Why not . . . . . . ?
2. Why a can? Why not . . . . . . ?
3. Why only a door lock? What about . . . . . . ?
4. Why a cord? What if you . . . . . . ?
5. Who are they fatiguing? Why not use . . . . . . ?

6.03 CREATE A NEW VIEWPOINT

Look at the drawing in Figure 6.2. What do you see?

Figure 6.2

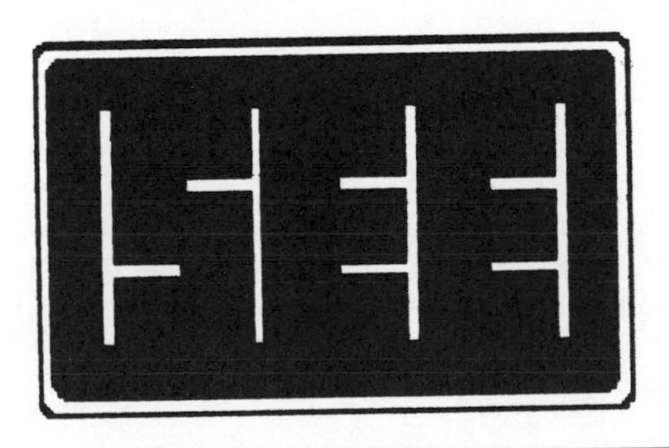

You have just experienced what psychologists refer to as figure-ground relationships. Because of the physical limitations of our brains, we only observe one stimulus set at a time when contrasted against another. We can't see both patterns at the same time.

If you had trouble seeing the word SEE in the drawing, you're not alone. Some people have to be guided, letter by letter, until they can make out the word. The other pattern is made up of the outlines of the letters.

To test your ability to switch back and forth between the two patterns, focus on the word, then on the background patterns in rapid succession. If you can do this easily, you have a well-developed mind. You're on the way to visual flexibility!

6.04 SWITCH AROUND

Flexibility also is the ability to observe rapid changes in visual figures. Quickly look over the top three drawings in Figure 6.3. Then select the one drawing (A, B, C, or D) that comes next in the series.

Figure 6.3 Which drawing comes next?

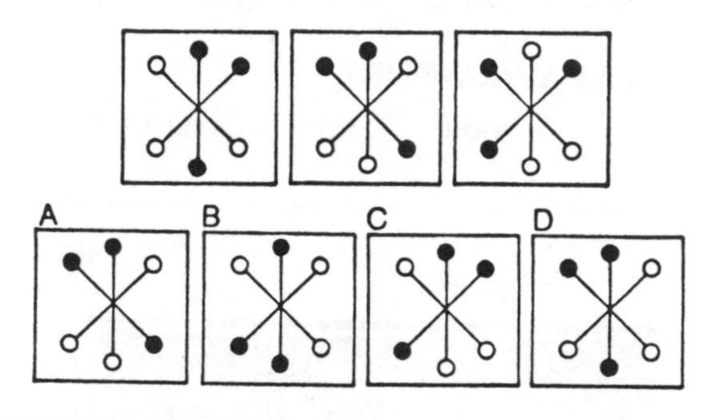

The ability to analyze and synthesize figural information quickly is one sign of a flexible right mind. To solve the problem, each line is rotated one place to the left. Thus, the correct answer is B.

6.05 SYMBOL RELATIVES

Being able to classify symbols according to similarities or differences helps develop new perspectives and teaches you to break away from conventional constraints. Categorizing information into related or unrelated categories is essential in all stages of creative problem solving. The more practice you have in this skill, the better equipped you are to attack unstructured situations.

List at least ten different ways that at least four groups of the symbols in Figure 6.4 are similar. For example, which ones contain or enclose other symbols? Which have straight lines? Only curved lines? Represent common shapes (waves, hourglass, clouds, etc.)?

6.06 SPY TELEGRAMS

Haven't you always wondered how well-developed your symbolic

Figure 6.4 How are the symbols similar?

redefinitional skills were? Haven't we all? Well, you can test them with this exercise.

We use symbols to communicate meaning. Sometimes the symbols we select to transmit are not received the way we intended. When this occurs, receivers must redefine the symbols in a way meaningful to them. Thus, we generate new perspectives to help us understand a message. The same is true during creative problem solving. We often must redefine a problem to create new perspectives.

In this exercise, you must redefine symbolic material to give it meaning. Your performance will depend on your symbolic redefinitional skills. So, now you'll know how well-developed your skills are in this area.

Assume you have intercepted ten telegrams from an enemy spy. Contained within each telegram are at least two secret code words. For example, in telegram six, one word is BUTTON, another is AGES. The word OWN, however, would not count, since it is not part of two or more consecutive words.

Locate at least two secret code words in each of the following telegrams.

1. SAW ARCHANGEL LEAVE TODAY.
2. CLIMB ON ROW QUICKLY.
3. FORGET BOMB AS TOO LATE.
4. WENT TO TIMBUKTU. LIP SORE.
5. LOST MY LIGHTER. UGANDA IS HOT.
6. TRUCK BROKE DOWN BUT TONNAGE STILL O.K.
7. PUT IT ON MY TAB. LEAVE THE RESTAURANT.
8. CANNOT FULFIL TERRIBLE EDICT.
9. SAW ONE ACRE. ATE A COW.
10. AM ON THE PAMPAS TO RALLY SUPPORT.

6.07 BREAKDOWN

By restructuring problems to achieve new perspectives, unique ways of dealing with problems can be revealed. The better we can do this, the easier it is to develop creative solutions. A one-sided view produces only conventional solutions.

The ability to pull apart problems requires practice and much persistence; the task is made more difficult by our self-imposed perceptual constraints. As noted by Charles Kettering, you can't see the view from the bottom of a rut. It's up to us to practice and persevere in climbing out of our ruts.

Look at Drawing A in Figure 6.5 and note the different ways it has been broken down, as shown in Figure 6.6 on the next page. You may notice other breakdowns in addition to the sample shown here. Do the same with drawings B and C.

If you have trouble with this exercise, keep trying. You may need to change your approach, for instance, darkening each line as you go along, until you have included all of the lines.

Figure 6.5 Drawings for the Breakdown Exercise.

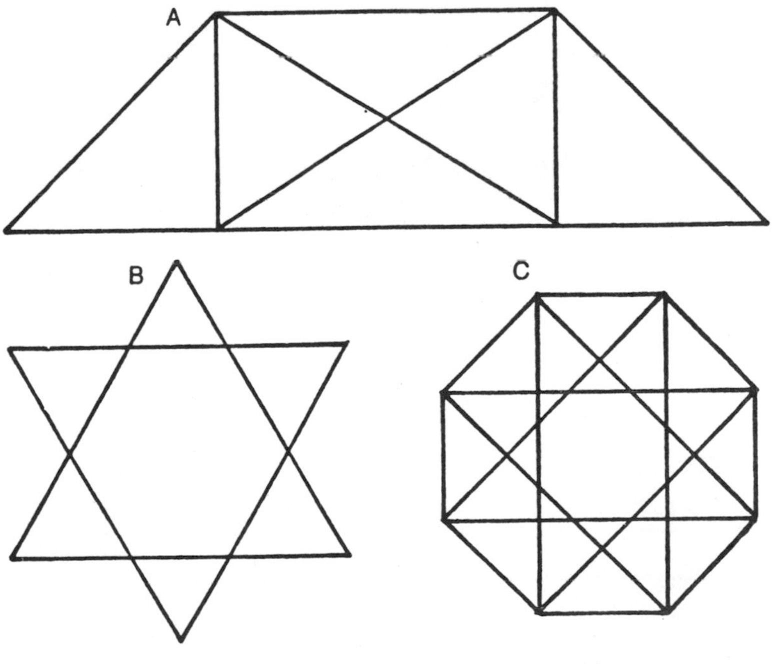

A

B

C

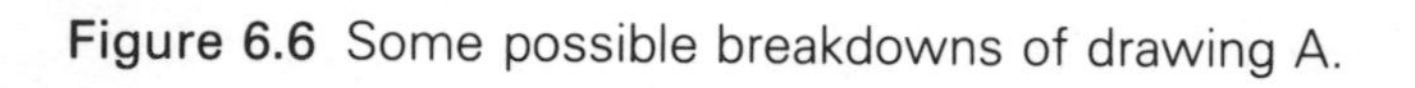

Figure 6.6 Some possible breakdowns of drawing A.

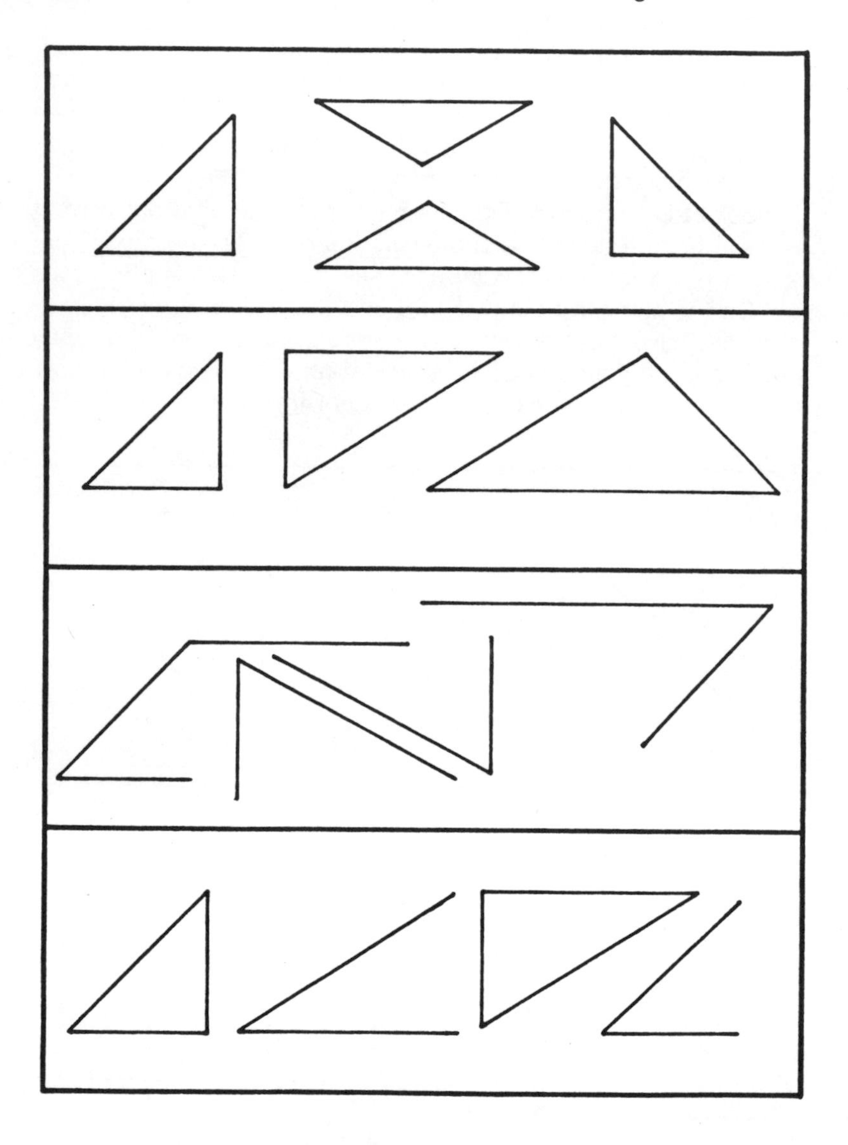

6.08 TAKE A STAND

This exercise also deals with your ability to visualize and analyze a situation. Figure out how you and another person can stand on one sheet of newspaper without being able to touch each other. Stepping off the paper is not allowed.

Some solutions: Place the newspaper under a door and close the door. The two people standing on either end of the paper are unable to touch each other. Or, inject both people with a paralyzing drug that prevents all movement. What other creative solutions can you find?

6.09 TAKE IT OFF

This classic problem is ideal for illustrating the necessity to view problems with a fresh eye. An open wine bottle is placed in the center of a small rug. The problem is to remove the bottle without spilling the wine or touching the bottle with any part of your body or any other object.

Possible solutions: Slowly begin rolling one end of the rug towards the center. When the roll of the rug reaches the bottle, it will gradually push it toward the other end until it slides off. Or, build a mold around the rug, cover the rug with a silicone gel, fill the mold with cement, and slide the rug from underneath the bottle. Now you try to think of other possibilities.

6.10 JUST LIKE THAT

Analogies are one of the most powerful tools for stimulating solutions. Looking for similarities among objects, ideas or relationships leads to the development of unique solutions.

Try developing analogies by completing the following statements. Don't be concerned that the analogous activities may not be "correct" or directly related to the statement. The purpose here is to gain a new perspective in order to break away from self-imposed constraints. The first three are done to get you started.

1. Brushing your teeth is like . . .
   - shining your shoes
   - scrubbing the kitchen floor

- polishing silver
- washing your car

2. Disposing of garbage is like . . .
   - getting a divorce
   - going to the bathroom
   - draining dirty bathwater
   - spitting
3. Saving energy is like . . .
   - putting money in the bank
   - storing fat in your body
   - being constipated
   - an athlete resting between races
4. Employee absenteeism is like . . .
5. Driving a car is like . . .
6. School vandalism is like . . .
7. Littering the highways is like . . .
8. Job dissatisfaction is like . . .
9. Painting a house is like . . .
10. Cleaning a house is like . . .

Now examine each analogy to see what solutions are suggested and try to develop a practical solution. This is known as a force fit. For example, saving energy is like putting money in the bank, because the energy can be stored when not needed and withdrawn when it is.

Many of us fail to take full advantage of the power in analogies and end up using direct analogies that result in conventional solutions. If possible, try to make your analogies as different as possible from the original statement.

6.11 SDRAWKCAB

One way to gain a new perspective on a problem is to reverse its initial statement and analyze it for solutions. If you were interested in improving a car's gas mileage, think of how you might DECREASE it.

In practicing this backwards way of looking at problems, remember that it's not how you reverse it that is important, but rather that you reverse the problem in as many different ways as possible.

For example, how can you make meetings more efficient? Possible reversals include how to make meetings more chaotic, how to make individuals more efficient, how to make them more inefficient. The solutions suggested in the reversal process might be: allowing time for unrestricted discussions, or airing grievances. Or a discussion on how individuals organize their time and activities might make a meeting more organized.

Try your hand at reversing the problems in these statements.

1. How to increase employee job satisfaction.
2. How to reduce street crime.
3. How to reduce or eliminate arson.
4. How to prevent football injuries.

6.12 WOULD YOU BELIEVE?

Distorting a problem situation is yet another way to provide new perspectives and develop unique solutions. Comedians rely heavily on distortion and exaggerations, stretching the facts about a situation in an unusual or unexpected manner.

In problem solving, when we list the objectives and then stretch each one, we are able to view the problem in a new way. The type of exaggeration is not important as much as is getting practice in this ability.

A problem of how to develop a better briefcase might be constructed thus:

Original Objective	Exaggerated Objective	Possible Solution
Lightweight	No weight	Use no metal; use self-reinforcing vinyl material
Easy to open	Always open	Opens on touch; use outside pockets
Secure from unauthorized entry	Opens only for owner	Voice-actuated locks

Here's a problem for you to practice: develop a better copying machine.

6.13 FANTASYLAND

To assume that anything and everything is possible is to break away from self-imposed constraints. When the mind is allowed the freedom to speculate, unique solutions can emerge.

A problem of how to prevent vandals from entering a school might be resolved by eliminating all windows. More practically, break-resistant glass could be used in the windows.

Take your own trip to fantasyland. Develop some fantasy solutions for these problems, including (if you can) some practical solutions.

1. How to reduce highway accidents.

   Fantasy: Eliminate all drivers.

   Practical: Install a buried cable beneath the highway to control traffic.

2. How to eliminate typing errors.

   Fantasy: Typewriter knows what you intend to do and self-corrects errors.

   Practical: Typewriter uses voice-actuated mechanism programmed to detect and correct errors.

3. How to prevent water damage to houses in flood-plain areas.
4. How to develop a carpet that never gets dirty.
5. How to prevent air loss in automobile tires.

6.14 SILLY INVENTIONS

Fantasy – stretching the mind beyond what is usually considered rational – can be valuable in creative problem solving. It promotes flexible thinking and gives us an opportunity to suspend judgment.

This exercise can be especially fun when done with a group of people who can make a game out of it by judging who's invention is the silliest. Remember, today's silly invention (e.g., dinners from a box) might be tomorrow's hot product idea (e.g., convenience foods).

An example of a silly idea would be a new type of bathroom scale that was capable of these things:

1. Whenever you step on it, you will weigh what you desire.
2. When you are overweight, it will say "ouch" when you step on it.
3. You find out your weight by placing the scale on your head.
4. If you start to eat something fattening, the scale will sound an alarm.
5. The scale will be so lightweight you can pack it in your suitcase.
6. The scale will give you a mild electrical shock if you're overweight.
7. It will automatically record every weight ever registered.

An example of a silly invention for you to play with might be a sound-wave machine that prevents household dust. Or an automobile that is capable of avoiding all traffic jams.

6.15 JUST SUPPOSE

We often block our thinking because we cannot overcome environmental constraints. If we imagine a different environment, constraints we normally face might be easier to overcome.

Just suppose everyone was restricted to a wheelchair and had the use of only one finger on one arm. How would life be different under these circumstances? What kind of homes would need to be designed? How would appliances have to be modified?

You might begin by describing all the different aspects of this home and activities that might be performed in it. For example, list doors, windows, televisions, lights, toilets, refrigerators, washers, etc. Then, consider the activities involved in using these items. Consider also entertainment activities, food preparation, and cleaning.

6.16 CUT IT UP

Imagine it is a holiday season and you live alone. Seven relatives are coming to your place to eat pie with you. You have one pie and very little time to cut it; in fact, you only have time to cut the pie into eight pieces using three cuts. Can you do it?

The original solution is shown in Figure 6.7 and it illustrates making an unwarranted assumption, such as assuming that the cuts must be straight and the pieces pie-shaped. Another solution is to cut the pie in half (from the top), stack one half on the other and cut this stack in half, and then stack this half upon the other and cut it in half. Once we test assumptions and become aware we're making them, creative solutions can flow.

Figure 6.7 Cut-up solutions.

Original solution

a

b

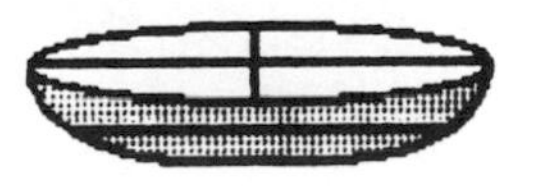

c

The interesting thing about this and similar exercises is that most of us have trouble thinking of even one solution. However, once we test unwarranted assumptions, solution quantity is limited only by our creativity.

6.17 FILL 'ER UP

Draw a circle about the size of a quarter. Fill in the circle using a pen or pencil.

Did you carefully avoid coloring outside of the lines? Most of us do, and we believe we satisfied the conditions of the exercise.

However, another satisfactory solution is shown in Figure 6.8.

Figure 6.8 Fill 'er up solutions.

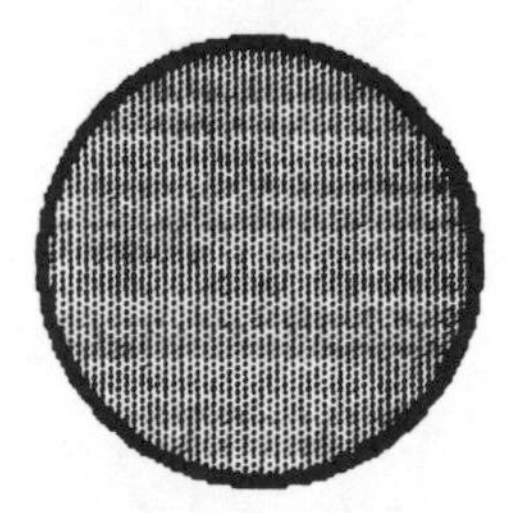

Yes, the coloring does go outside the lines of the circle and no, it doesn't look very neat. But if you reread the instructions, you'll see nothing is said about HOW you should fill in the circle nor about neatness as a criterion.

Neatness is a conditioned response here, for we were all trained in school to color within the lines. Although it is important to stay within the lines during some activities that require neatness, this constraint can be counterproductive when creative solutions are required. When you think about one "correct" solution, you limit yourself and your opportunities.

6.18 DOTS THE WAY

Connect the dots shown in Figure 6.9. What type of figure is formed?

Figure 6.9 Connect the dots.

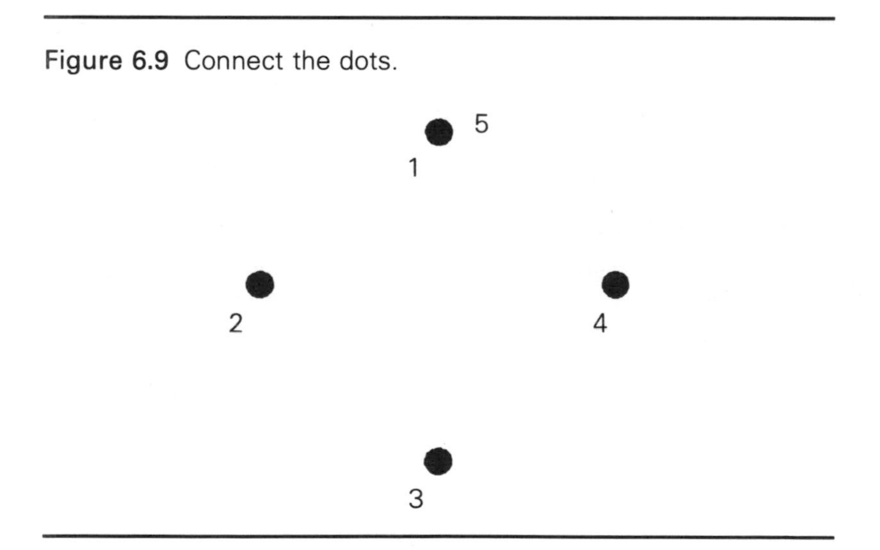

The answer is . . . a diamond. But ask yourself, why did you follow the numbers? The problem said nothing about following the numbers, which in this case were extraneous to the problem and represented data you could ignore or use. If you ignored the numbers, an unlimited number of figures could result.

Conditioning has struck again. Useful in some cases, such blind obedience restricts creative ideas.

6.19 LETTER LINE-UP

What are the next three letters in the sequence below?

AEF	HIK
BCD	GJO

If you had trouble here, it may have been because you were seeking a sequence based on the letters being placed in alphabetical order with alternating groups of three above or below the line.

Look again. All letters that contain only straight lines are above the line.

Letters with curved lines are below. Thus, the next three letters "must" be LMN. Unless of course you defined the problem's constraints differently than I did . . .

Problem analysis calls for awareness of existing patterns and relationships among variables. To break patterns and achieve creative insights, you first must be aware of what patterns exist. Once you analyze how the patterns interact and affect perceptions, solutions often pop right out.

6.20 PAPER WALTZ

Using a legal-size sheet of paper, cut or tear a hole large enough to walk through. There is more than one solution to this problem.

Although this problem may appear to defy solution, one is possible if you test assumptions. One key assumption involves the word "hole." What is a hole and how do you make one? A broader definition is an opening.

Test another assumption. Must you use the paper as it is? Or, may you modify it or use it differently? One approach would be to think of the paper as material for an opening. Simply cut along the lines and connect the ends to form a "hole" large enough to walk through as in Figure 6.10.

You might have thought of other solutions, such as testing the assumption about "walking through." Did you assume it must be a person who walks through the hole?

6.21 STRIP TEASE

Tear a letter-size sheet of paper into thirds, lengthwise. Make one

Figure 6.10 Possible solution for Paper Waltz.

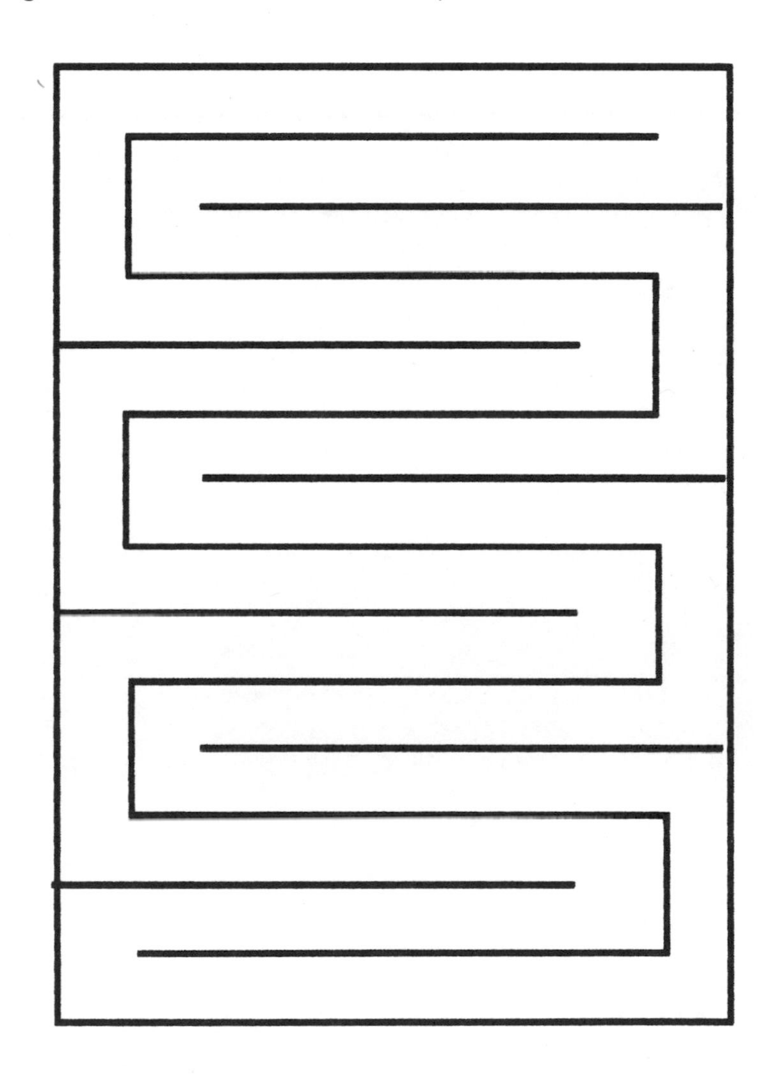

tear from top to bottom, but leave about two inches untorn at the bottom. Make a second tear from bottom to top, and leave about two inches untorn at the top. Both tears should be about 9″ long.

Now for the problem to try: grasp each of the outer strips in one of your hands. Pull the strips in opposite directions so that the middle strip falls out.

Again, a logical or obvious solution will not work here. Be wary of unwarranted assumptions, such as assuming that both strips are joined with equal strength. If you try to tear the paper by grasping both ends, the middle strip will stay attached to one of the other strips. One possibility is to hold the center strip between your teeth while pulling the other strips apart.

7

Letting Go

Pick up a pen or pencil and, without making any evaluations, think of ten different uses for it other than writing. Allow one minute for this. Don't read any further until you have done it.

Finished? Did you think of ten uses within the time period? I asked you to do this to test how much power I could wield through the written word. If you compiled without reading further, I'd now like you to send me one hundred dollars. Just kidding. Honest. (Then again . . .)

The REAL reason was to demonstrate ideational fluency – the ability to generate large numbers of ideas with relative ease. Creative solutions cannot be judged by their correctness, so a large number of solutions must be generated to increase the odds of finding one that works. The better you are at rapidly producing ideas, the more likely you are to develop creative solutions.

Other types of fluency, such as word and associational, are similar to ideational in that they involve generating ideas. Word fluency is the rapid generation of words according to some specified requirement, such as words containing the letter R. Associational fluency uses rapid generation of words within a prescribed set of meanings – for example, a listing of synonyms.

Most of the exercises in this chapter are representative of the three types of fluency just described. We are going to break format here and have you perform the exercises rapidly, one after the other, leaving the evaluations for later.

7.01 BRAIN GUSHER

Before you begin this exercise, get as relaxed as you can, temporarily ridding yourself of any problems bothering you. Take several deep breaths. Inhale through your nose and exhale through your mouth. Feel the tension drain away.

Cover up all but the first word in this list. Look at the word and write down the first three words that come to mind. Write them down as fast as you can think of them. Uncover the second word and do the same thing. Continue until you have used all fifty words.

hope	red	tape	wood	laugh
star	square	rocket	money	paper
glass	dry	flower	egg	silly
early	book	cork	horse	train
never	menace	happy	out	snow
pig	free	fence	fat	walk
card	water	old	hard	late
light	yesterday	near	cold	above
dog	balloon	ride	ant	cow
moon	elbow	mountain	rough	help

7.02 PREFIX-IT

As rapidly as possible, list as many words as you can think of in two minutes that begin with the prefix DIS. Now do the same for the prefixes ANTI and CON.

7.03 LETTER HUNT

Within two minutes, list as many words as possible that contain the letter G. Now do the same for the letters K and P, allowing two minutes for each list.

7.04 UNDERWEIGHT

Within three minutes list everything you can think of that weighs less than a pound.

7.05 WORD CHAINS

Using the following word clusters, try to think of at least two different objects that each cluster could describe.

1. metal, hinged, attaches
2. wire, talk, plastic
3. paper, glue, ink
4. keys, rubber, letters

5. fabric, foam, floor
6. dirt, green, water
7. soft, white, paper
8. rectangular, flat, metal

7.06 SNIFF OUT

Thousands of people suffer, as I do, from allergies, and receive desensitizing injections of medicine drawn from small glass vials. I used to receive two injections every week and used up about one hundred of these little bottles every year. If five thousand other people do the same, that amounts to a half-million bottles each year, most of which were probably discarded.

If similar waste occurs with other products, the amount of energy consumed to produce such disposables must be staggering. Help me solve this problem by doing the following.

Think of (sniff out) how many different ways these bottles might be used once they have been emptied of their contents. A drawing of one such bottle, along with relevant information, is shown below.

Figure 7.1 Specifications for allergy medicine vials.

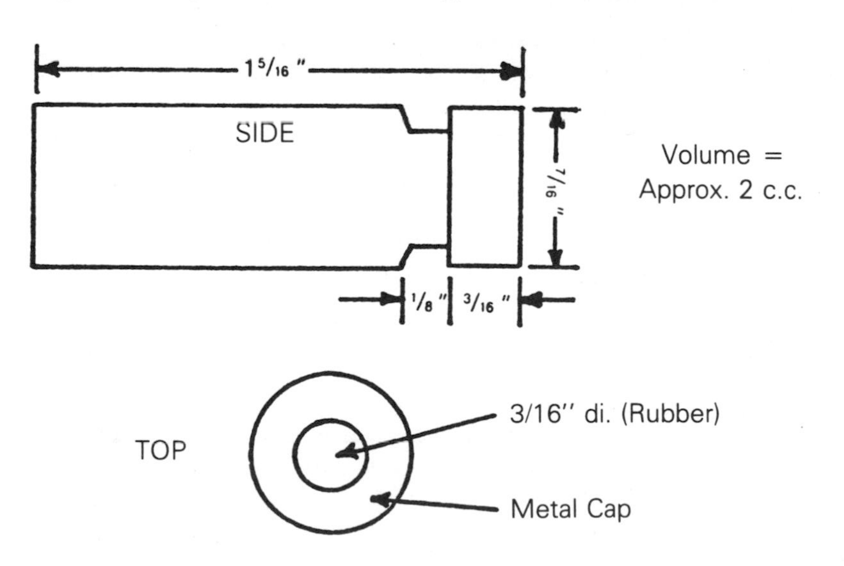

7.07 WORD RELATIVES

For each of the words that follow, think of as many synonyms as you can. Allow one minute for each word.

shout	hit
even	make
decide	see

7.08 GAR • BÄGÉ

Select five items that can be found in a wastebasket or garbage can. Generate ten uses for each item as fast as you can. Don't worry about silliness or practicality. Be concerned only with generating the ideas as rapidly as possible.

7.09 GO TO CLASS

In this exercise, instead of randomly listing uses for objects, list only uses that belong to a particular class. For instance, uses for a red brick might involve such classes as construction, weights, or support systems. As quickly as you can, list classes of use and actual uses for a wire coat hanger. List the class first, followed by its uses. Then go on to the next class, continuing until you run out of classes.

7.10 DON'T FORGET

A mnenomic device is something that is used to help memorize lists of data or information. A usual way to do this is to take the first letter of the first word for each item and construct a sentence. For example: memorize a grocery list by constructing a sentence from potato, celery, sugar, eggs: "Please Call Sam Early."

Practice your fluency skills by constructing as many different sentences as you can from the word MNEMONIC. Do this rapidly for five minutes. Silly sentences are fine, since they're usually easier to recall.

7.11 COLUMN RELATIVES

From the columns below, select one word from each column. Then identify as many things as possible that possess these two attributes. For instance, hot and mobile might suggest a hair dryer, or the sun.

Try at least ten different two-word combinations. Once you have mastered these, use one word from the first column and two words from the second.

hot	mobile
cold	silvery
large	wooden
small	metallic
fast	electrical
slow	glass
square	slippery
round	rough
expensive	transparent
inexpensive	flexible

7.12 JUST ALIKE, ONLY DIFFERENT

See how many different areas of commonality you can find for the words that follow. Begin by gradually seeking common areas between pairs of words. Then progress by adding one word at a time until you are working with at least four different words. Any combination will do, so don't feel restricted by rows or columns. As an example, a dime and a rug both can be rolled; an egg, window and flower all can be easily broken.

dime	tree	square	telephone
book	window	bucket	paint
airplane	city	pencil	rug
egg	garden	flashlight	flower

7.13 IT CAME FROM BENEATH THE BLOT

Using the ink-blot pattern shown in Figure 7.2 on the next page, make up ten possibilities for a movie the pattern might represent.

7.14 WHAT'S IN A NAME?

Have you ever heard of a janitor whose job title is Custodial Engineer? A teacher named a Language Skills Coordinator? A store clerk who is a Goods Exchange Facilitator? Practice your associational fluency by making up the silliest or most bureaucratic-sounding titles for these occupations.

plumber	dentist	disc jockey
baker	lawyer	house painter
doctor	bus driver	undertaker

Figure 7.2 Ink blot for developing movie titles.

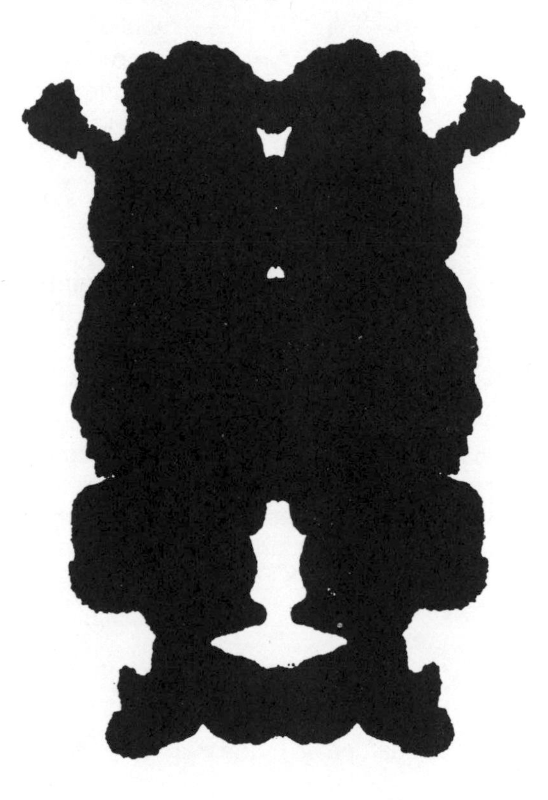

7.15 SPY STORIES

Using at least one secret code from each telegram in the Spy Telegrams exercise (Chapter 6, page 82), write a brief spy story. To make things a bit more interesting, use the words in the order in which they appeared in the different telegrams. Don't spend a lot of time on this exercise. Let your thoughts flow naturally.

7.16 IT TAKES TWO

When we perceive a problem, we often use the first definition that comes to mind. This definition can either prompt or hinder a creative solution.

A technique known as the "two words" method (Olson, 1980) ensures a more productive definition, forcing you to consider other meanings for the action verb and object in your definition. You continually redefine the problem through different verb and object combinations, then use the combinations as stimuli for generating ideas.

For instance, suppose your problem is: In what ways might I improve (action verb) indoor air quality (object)? First, list similar or related words for the verb and object.

Improve	Air Quality
advance	inhalation
better	atmosphere
enhance	breeze
upgrade	breath

Next, examine different combinations to suggest ideas. Don't judge the ideas now.

1. Use fans continuously (advance - breath).
2. Improve air filtration systems (better - inhalation).
3. Fragrance in air system (enhance - atmosphere).
4. Ensure house insulation isn't too air tight (upgrade - breeze).

Now you try it by determining in what ways you might:

1. reduce stress in your life?
2. better save money?
3. increase your job satisfaction?

7.17 ALPHABET ASSOCIATIONS

This exercise adds two twists we haven't used before. First, instead of free associating in any way possible, you must generate related words. Second and most challenging, your lists must be in alphabetical order. As fast as you can, alphabetically list related words for:

sports   foods   cars

7.18 FUNNY KNIFE

An exercise in Tom Wujec's *Pumping Ions* can be modified as a fluency test. A woman goes into a room and gets a glass of water.

She drinks the water and holds her breath for about thirty seconds. She glances at a mirror and sees the reflection of a man behind her with a knife ready to stab her. As he lowers the knife, she screams. Then they laugh.

Describe what is happening. List as many possibilities as you can.

COMMENTS AND SAMPLE RESPONSES

Now that you have performed the exercises, let's take a look at what they did for you and what your responses tell you.

7.01 BRAIN GUSHER

A clogged up brain is a serious drawback to generating ideas. The ability to let go and allow the rapid flow of ideas doesn't come easily when the mind is blocked by censors that are geared to screening out right from wrong.

Did you have trouble with this exercise, stumbling to think of words, or did they flow easily? If you hesitated much, your censors were getting in the way. It might take practice to do this exercise effortlessly.

Also consider why you chose the words you did. They may be a clue to your experiential background and may provide you with insight into how you come up with such ideas.

7.02 PREFIX-IT

This is an exercise in word fluency. How many of these (or different) words did you list?

disassociate
disapprove
disappear
disallow
disappoint
discourage
disband
disarm
disable
disadvantage
disagree
disassemble
disavow
discard
discharge
antibiotic
antibody
anticlimax
antidote
antifreeze
antihistamine
antimatter
antipasto
antipathy
antiquated
antiseptic
antisocial
antithesis
antitoxic
antiestablishment
contract
concave
conceal

concede	concentric	concession
conceit	concept	conciliate
conceive	concern	concise
concentrate	concert	conclude

7.03 LETTER HUNT

If most or all of your words began with the specified letter, try the exercise again. Only this time, use words in which the specified letter is not the first letter of the word. To make it harder, avoid words that rhyme.

After doing the exercise, recall how you prompted your mind to think of the words. You probably had an easier time with the exercise if you used a system, such as looking at the objects in your immediate environment or progressing through the alphabet.

7.04 UNDERWEIGHT

Here's a list of items typically generated by persons doing this exercise:

butterfly	checkbook	canary
comb	hummingbird	strand of hair
feather	button	pen
shoelace	pencil	paper clip
leaf	blade of grass	sheet of paper
watch	sock	tie
envelope	stamp	sugar cube
grain of salt	piece of bread	light bulb
eraser	pillow	playing card
staple	tissue	driver's license

If you didn't list at least thirty different items, consider how you sought ideas. One way to increase your fluency is to think of classes of objects. In the list above, the class of FOOD would include sugar cube, grain of salt, piece of bread. If you want to practice some more, try listing fifty or more different items, without duplicating your previous lists.

7.05 WORD CHAINS

Associational fluency is an important aspect of creativity. This exercise helps you make connections among words, even though unrelated, to describe another word.

1. Stapler, door
2. Telephone, walkie-talkie, tape recorder
3. Book, party hat, envelope, decorated paper straw
4. Typewriter, typesetting machine, initialed key ring with rubber decoration
5. Chair, couch or floor pillow

7.06 SNIFF OUT

How many ideas were you able to generate? If you had trouble thinking of ideas, try the exercise again in this manner.

First write down all the uses you can think of within five minutes. Then go do something else for about ten minutes. Return and list ideas for another five minutes.

Were your ideas unique the second time? If you begin to run out of ideas, try these suggestions:

1. Analyze the bottle according to its essential characteristics: shape, size, volume, material. Can these characteristics be used separately or in combination with other products or materials to produce something new? Thinking about the shape may lead to using the bottle as a guide for drawing circles; the volume might point to a place for biological cultures.

2. Beware of placing unnecessary constraints on your thinking. Instead of thinking of ways to use the bottle, what about developing ideas for using quantities of glass, metal and rubber? Although the bottle in its entirety could be used as a milk bottle for a dollhouse, you could use the glass parts for beaded curtains, the rubber for fishing floats, the metal to hang Christmas tree ornaments.

3. Focus on one characteristic of the bottle and develop an analogy. For example, does inserting the syringe make you think of other things that could be inserted? Consider inserting lengths of wire and turn the bottles into earrings.

7.07 WORD RELATIVES

The ability to think of words having some relation to one another is known as associational fluency. Here are some examples you might have listed:

Shout: cry out, hoot, exclaim, vociferate, yell

Even: level, flat, smooth, regular, steady, equal, balanced

Decide: determine, settle, resolve, purpose, conclude

7.08 GAR • BÄGÉ

If you did this exercise quickly, you're probably very good at ideational fluency. Some possibilities include:

TIN CAN: pencil or paintbrush holder, pot for small plants, cement mold, toy telephone, dollhouse roof, birdhouse

FOIL: sun reflector, cooking, birdcage liner, TV antenna, space suit for mice, insulated socks, disco bathing suit

PAPER NAPKINS: paper hat, parachute for mice, placemats, earmuffs, portable toilet for pigeons, pooper scooper, attache case for ferrets

7.09 GO TO CLASS

Using five classes, the first three list possible uses for a coat hanger. You might then try using the last two classes, if you didn't already use them.

FOOD: shish kebab, hot dogs, marshmallows, chestnuts, popcorn holder

HOLDING THINGS: key rings, flowerpots, hanging pictures, spools of thread, bucket handle, plants, fish stringer, shoe rack, tie rack, kitchen utensils

DECORATIONS: mobiles, bracelet, tree ornaments, wreaths, sculptures, earrings

HOLDING IN HANDS:

REPAIRS:

7.10 DON'T FORGET

Meet Nat Every Monday Over New Income Costs.
Maybe Nellie Eats Moose On Naked Indian Calves.
Must Newton Eat Money Over Nancy's Ice Cupboard?
Missiles Need Energy Material Or Nuclear Incidents Collapse.
Move Near Every Mother On Narcotics In Cans.

7.11 COLUMN RELATIVES

This exercise is designed to help you develop associational fluency. Here are some ideas:

large-wooden: a tree, a building, a wooden sculpture, a wooden bridge

small-metallic: a dime, a paper clip, a thumbtack

square-slippery: a newly waxed floor tile, a wet sidewalk, a block of ice

expensive-transparent: a diamond, crystal stemware, gasoline

7.12 JUST ALIKE, ONLY DIFFERENT

The ability to develop common associations among apparently unrelated objects is an important creative thinking skill. Recognition of such common associations leads to creative solutions.

Here are just a few of the commonalities possible, using two, three or four word combinations:

dime-tree: both are round, have rough outer edges, can be recycled, are capable of growing in value over time

pencil-rug-flower: all three are or can be made of natural materials, can be found in a house, can be used for decorating purposes

city-square-telephone-dime: all four involve exchanges between or among people, are relevant to the communications media, and have prescribed boundaries.

7.13 IT CAME FROM BENEATH THE BLOT

Being able to assign labels to ambiguous material provides a useful exercise in mental fluency. Although originality is required, the ease with which you can produce labels gives a fair indication of your mental fluency. Imagine seeing a movie entitled: They Wore Poodles On Their Heads, or Journey Into The Void, Bonzo Gets a Hickey, Saga of the Gorilla Janitors, Mating of the Platypuses.

If you found yourself using only one perspective (for instance, people with things on their heads), your fluency level was greatly diminished. To make full use of the stimuli provided, turn the blot and view it from different angles, or switch back and forth from the figure-ground relationships presented by the dark and white contrasts.

The same principle applies when you are faced with an unstructured problem. You must be able to view it from many different perspectives in order to produce unique solutions.

7.14 WHAT'S IN A NAME?

It seems that many bureaucrats have a highly-developed associational fluency, since they are able to replace simple, easily-understood names with more complex and vague titles.

Here are some examples of silly bureaucratic ideas:

PLUMBER: suction supervisor, tube technician, faucet facilitator, flushologist

DISC JOCKEY: flatter-platter player, spinologist, aural augmenter, disc dealer

UNDERTAKER: permanent-resident specialist, rigor mortis manager, corpus planter, plot-placement analyst

7.15 SPY STORIES

To test your originality and ability in making associations between words, compare your story with this one:

WAR is never pleasant, Harry thought as he made his way to George's tent to BORROW a razor blade. In the tent, Harry pulled up a stool, sat down and moistened his LIPS.

"Did you find out who shot K.R.?" he said as he eyed the top BUTTON on George's coat. George replied, "No, we haven't been able to determine when he was shot."

"Well, we know that he did BLEED to death, as we first thought."

George looked surprised. "Do you think someone has tried to CREATE the impression that he had not bled to death?"

Harry nodded and looked PAST George to the blood-stained razor on the dresser. "Yeah, I'm sure that's what happened, and it wasn't the PASTOR who did it."

7.16 IT TAKES TWO

Some possible two word lists for the problem statements are:

1. In what ways might you reduce stress in your life?

Reduce	Stress
diminish	anxiety
downgrade	pressures
lower	distress
dilute	apprehension

Sample: Avoid taking on more jobs than you can handle (dilute - pressures).

2. In what ways might you better save money?

Save	Money
economic	bucks
recycle	dollars
conserve	assets

Sample: Conduct garage sales and put the proceeds into a savings account (recycle-assets).

7.17 ALPHABET ASSOCIATIONS

This exercise is designed to enhance associational fluency. We've started them for you.

Sports: baseball, basketball, boxing, football, g . . . .

Foods: apples, bread, carrots, cheese, grapes, l . . . .

Cars: Alpha-Romero, Buick, Chevrolet, Dodge, F . . . .

7.18 FUNNY KNIFE

According to Mr. Wujec, the correct answer is that the woman has the hiccups. Probably the man is trying to scare her and stop the hiccups. Other possible explanations:

This is really a scene in a play.

She is having a nightmare or hallucinating on drugs.

They are simply clowning around.

They belong to a religious cult and the woman is being sacrificed.

She's taking a self-defense course; he is helping her practice her skills.

He really is trying to kill her. They both happen to suffer from a laughing disorder during times of high stress.

A prankster sprayed laughing gas in their faces.

Being Different

Originality is one aspect of creativity about which many of us feel the least confident. We naturally tend to compare others' creativity with our own and may find ourselves lacking in comparison. We sometimes have an unrealistic standard for ourselves, not realizing that each of us is unique and creative in our own way.

If we all were alike in our originality, then no one would be unique or original. We should cherish our own uniqueness and not try to be someone we're not. But do try to build on and increase your own creativity. Forget what everyone else can do. Learn basic skills from others, but then go off on your own to make your own little contribution to the world.

The exercises in this chapter provide an opportunity to practice your originality in figural elaboration, product modifications and improvements, symbolic redefinitions, development of new names, and story completions.

Don't be too concerned with how unique your responses might be. Your major goal here is to express your originality to the fullest extent possible. You are trying to train YOUR creative mind, not someone else's, so don't wonder whether someone else could do the exercises better.

8.01 STEAMING IDEAS

Do you ever get steamed over irritants in your environment? Like a telephone that slides all over the place while you're using it and then falls to the floor just as you are proposing marriage to that special someone? Or what about those "easy-to-open" packages?

Make a list of things in your environment that really get you steamed and then select five items that bug you the most. What improvements could be made? For example, could the "resealable" wax paper in cereal boxes be connected to the box top so it stays folded when not in use? Think of as many different solutions as you can for each of your five items.

Bug List	Possible Solutions
Shoes that don't quite fit	Use a material that conforms to the human foot. After wearing for a while, it can be "locked in" to the shape of your foot.
Childproof pill bottle	Use a combination dial. Turn cap to specified numbers and cap comes off.
Toys sealed in molded plastic containers	
Grass that sticks to the underside of lawn mowers	

8.02 FILL-OUT

Many problems present only partial information to us. We need to develop our ability to build on incomplete information, especially for unstructured problems. This exercise will give you practice in visual elaboration of figures. Keep in mind that the unconventional response is likely to be the most creative. Complete the following figures:

8.03 DRAW-A-WORD

We usually communicate our thoughts in words and, much less often, in pictures. We could communicate more vividly if we used both words and pictures. Practice using your originality by making pictures out of words. Here are two examples, using the words "cup" and "hole."

Now try it yourself with these words: cash, telephone, radio, elevators. For additional practice, make pictures of as many words as you can from the following paragraph:

The letter arrived by airmail on Thursday. It offers the first look at the administration's priorities as the university prepares to trim its budget needs to meet expected levels of funding.

8.04 PICTURE THAT

The ability to depict information in different forms is valuable to creative problem solving. Test this aspect of your creativity with this exercise.

You have been commissioned to produce information signs for an international exhibit of new products. You need to develop symbols that point out the location of the exhibits, and that are easily understood by everyone, no matter their country or language. An example for restrooms could be:

(Men)

(Women)

The major product areas to be dealt with in this exercise are: computers, telephones, bicycles, airplanes, automobiles, sailboats and tanks.

8.05 SOMETHING NEW

The different characteristics of ideas often suggest new ideas, objects or improvements. For this exercise, select an object or idea, break it down by describing its features, and then modify the features to suggest something new. A hand-held egg beater could be broken down and modified like this:

1. handle trigger grip, lengthen with counterweights
2. crank make larger

3. gears increase ratio
4. beaters coat with nonstick substance

Try doing this for your own objects or ideas.

8.06 GRID LOCK

A systematic method often used to generate ideas is based on the principle of forced relationships. It involves forcing together two or more objects or ideas to produce new ones, or using object characteristics to produce new ideas.

From the grid in Figure 8.1 (page 118), select an object from the first column and then one of the two attributes from each of the remaining columns. Using the attributes you selected, develop a new variation of the object.

Here's an example to get you started. Using a chair as the object, the following attributes might be selected.

wood	multipurpose	plastic	wide
long	soft	round	comes apart
light	electrical	tall	many colors

The chair you could design has a wooden frame with pliable plastic seats, is relatively long for tall people, and has rounded edges and is light-weight to allow it to be moved easily. It can be easily disassembled and has many uses supported by electrical devices, such as a drink dispenser or a muscle massager.

8.07 LABEL IT

Labels play an important role in creativity since they either restrict or enlarge our perceptual boundaries. We call a plane figure with four equal sides at right angles to each other a square (Figure 8.2).

However, we also can represent a square by the space it occupies: instead of drawing lines, we can fill in the space surrounding the lines (Figure 8.3). Now we have a SQUARINOUT, a bounded and unbounded space separated by a pattern traditionally known as a square.

If we always call a square a square, we limit ourselves in the conceptual tools we bring to problem solving.

Figure 8.1 Grid for producing object variations.

OBJECTS

Chair	Table	Ladder	Bookcase	Lamp	Bed	Workbench	Desk	ATTRIBUTES
								Metal Wood
								Glass Plastic
								Long Short
								Round Square
								Light Heavy
								Tall Short
								Movable Fixed
								Single-purpose Multi-purpose
								Narrow Wide
								Hard Soft
								Comes apart Unitary
								Electrical Nonelectrical
								One color Many colors

Figure 8.2 A Square.

Figure 8.3 Example of a Squarinout.

What other names can you think of for a square, a rectangle, a pyramid or a hexagon? To do this, think of the different ways these shapes can be constructed.

8.08 LIGHT UP YOUR LIFE

The method of forced relationships has been widely used to produce new variations of a product or idea. Forced relationships is where you take an object or idea unrelated to the one you want to modify and force them together to suggest something new.

A light bulb might be put together with a chair to suggest a glass or bulb-shaped chair. Modify the products listed below, using a light bulb as the unrelated object.

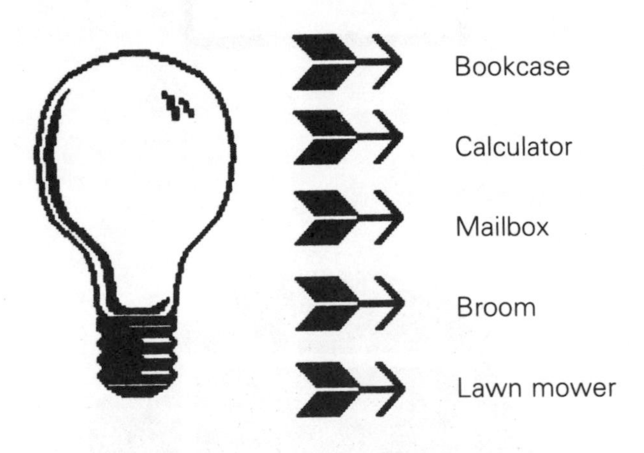

To prompt ideas, you might first list all relevant characteristics of a light bulb: glass, screw action, uses electricity, easily turned on and off, glows. Such a list also will help you break away from self-imposed constraints about a light bulb.

Here are a few possible solutions for each object:

BOOKCASE: sliding glass doors, electrically opened doors

MAILBOX: transparent to see mail, lights up when mail has arrived

CALCULATOR: screws into a pen, is disposable

BROOM: doubles as a flashlight, handle unscrews for easy storage

LAWN MOWER: transparent glass tank to tell when empty, inexpensive

8.09 WORD TO WORD

One way to produce new ideas is to reverse the procedure where an idea is developed and then named. Try starting with a name and then develop ideas from it. Use the words you formed from the Bunny Hop exercise in Chapter 4 to develop a new invention. Following are some examples from words you might have formed:

RABBIT	Rat, brat, bait, bra
MULTIPLY	Lip, pull, tulip, pill

Rat-Tulip:	a new breed of tulip that "eats" household flies
Ball-Pill:	a new bait form for fishing
Bra-Pull:	a quick release brassiere

8.10 NAME THAT EXERCISE

Develop a new name for all of the exercises in Chapters Four through Ten. Don't think too long on any one, but be spontaneous and as original as possible. For example:

Chapter Number	Current Name	Possible New Name
Three	Triadic Deeds	Bragging Rights
	On Purpose	Your Bent
Four	Mind Mapping	Brain Patterns
	Name That Letter	Alphabet Hunt
Five	Your Room	Know Your Space
	The Picnic	Eating Out
Six	Spy Telegrams	Secret Messages
	Just Like That	Almost The Same
Seven	It Takes Two . . .	Word Duals
	Alphabet Associations	Association Relations
	Funny Knife	Died Laughing

These are only examples. You should try the exercise with all of the titles.

8.11 THE MASTER

Ralph entered the large, marble-filled room. At the other end sat The Master. He seemed deep in thought, contemplating the mysteries of the universe. As Ralph drew closer he could sense the piercing eyes that seemed capable of cutting through one's soul yet embracing one warmly at the same time.

At the foot of the Master's ornately carved wooden perch, Ralph waited for a sign that he could speak. The Master looked away and cleared his throat. Taking this for the sign, Ralph began, "Master . . . " but was cut off as The Master raised his hand to signal silence. "Wrong sign," thought Ralph. Then The Master began to speak, "Yes, what do you want already?" With these words of encouragement, Ralph stammered and then blurted out the words that had haunted him for so many years. "Master, why have we been placed here on earth?"

With eyes that had witnessed almost a century of the human drama, The Master lowered his gaze to the floor and spoke nothing for five minutes. Then, as if by divine inspiration, he raised his eyes and looked directly at Ralph. "Crumbs," he said, and as he did, a wry smile formed at the corners of his mouth.

What did The Master mean by "crumbs"? . . .

8.12 END IT ALL

Write a humorous ending for the story that follows. This exercise also can provide entertainment as a game when several others are involved. For example, after everyone has described an ending, the most humorous one could be selected and the person awarded a prize.

Greg stealthily crept down the long corridor as the shadows from the wall torches danced lightly around him. It was cold and he wished that he had worn his long underwear. On his last two missions he had worn his long johns, only to find himself sweltering in some tropical climate. "Oh well," he thought, "life is knowing how to go on when you don't have your favorite pair of long johns."

Just then, his excursion into the deep philosophical issues of life was interrupted by a long, piercing scream, "Arrrrrrgh!" He paused momentarily and sharpened his senses. Even without his long johns, he felt his legs begin to perspire and his pulse quicken. "What could that horrifying scream mean?" he thought. Had he finally found what he was sent to find?

"I must be careful now," he said to himself. The slightest error could make the difference between success and failure.

He padded quietly to the end of the corridor, where he was met by a large, wooden door. Instead of a conventional doorknob, however, this door had a large cast-iron ring for a handle. Before pulling on the ring, he paused. "What if the door creaks like in one of those B movies?" Well, that was just a risk he would have to take. Grasping the ring, he tugged with all his might. No creak. The door didn't budge. It was then he saw the other decorative rings that also looked like door handles. So, *pushing* the door open, he peered inside. It was then he first heard the voices.

As the sliver of light from the partially opened door bounced off the walls of the corridor, Greg strained to hear the voices. They were laughing, but only the laughs of someone who has just committed or was about to commit some heinous deed. Pushing the door open further, he peered in and saw for the first time what he had most feared. This is what he had come to find. For inside the room, he saw . . .

8.13 NASAL NONSENSE

This is another exercise for practicing originality. Your task: Write a humorous ending for the following story.

Eye overlooking nose.

Cora looked up from her receptionist's desk at the Newtown Nasal Clinic just in time to see Dr. Sid Septum open the door to the supply room, cast a furtive glance up and down the hall, and quietly slip inside, closing the door behind him. She thought nothing of it, as the doctor often had to obtain nasal supplies from the room. However, when Nurse Sally Spray entered the room a few minutes later, her suspicions were aroused.

The good doctor and the nurse had been meeting like this for several months, and Cora was becoming more and more indignant. Sure, maybe her own nose was a little too small. But it was a nice nose. Her entire family had been cursed with small noses and she had almost resigned herself to her fate until she had met Dr. Snaffle several years ago.

She had been eating lunch one day near the bottom of the Spanish Steps in Rome when she had to blow her nose. Taking out a clean handkerchief from her purse, she carefully blew her nose. At almost the same moment, an attractive couple came walking down the steps and the man tripped over Cora's sack lunch. As he bent over to help her pick up the spilled contents, their eyes met and then their noses almost touched – her small protuberance and his more normal, elongated nose.

"Hi. I'm Harry Snaffle and I guess I've ruined your lunch. Would you care to join us? We were just on our way to have lunch ourselves."

Instinctively shrinking from his gesture of kindness because of her inferior nose, she hesitated and then reluctantly accepted. The pigeons were now beginning to gather around her spilled lunch, and she was still hungry. So Cora introduced herself to Dr. Snaffle, Dr. Snaffle introduced Cora to his companion, Sally Spray, and they began walking together.

There was something about Sally that Cora didn't like. It could have been the way she seemed to look down her nose at Cora when she greeted her. Or it could have been the menacing way Sally seemed to peer into her eyes. Cora made a mental note to try and figure out later what it was about Sally that disturbed her.

Meanwhile, they continued to stroll along in the noonday sun. Soon they began to cross over the Bridge of Angels, and it was there Cora first noticed Dr. Snaffle's magnificent profile.

For there silhouetted against the background of St. Peter's cathedral, was the biggest nose she had ever seen.

She continued to marvel at his nose over lunch and barely said a word the entire time. So she was taken by surprise when Dr. Snaffle offered her the receptionist's job at his nasal clinic back in the states.

While at her new job one day, Cora reminisced about her chance meeting with Dr. Snaffle and Nurse Spray. She decided it was time she took some action in regard to what she considered to be outrageous behavior on the part of Dr. Septum and Sally Spray.

She rose from her desk, smoothed down the wrinkles on her dress, and picked up her purse. Opening it, she rummaged around inside, pushed aside the handkerchiefs and nose sprays, and located her compact. Removing it from her purse, she opened it and took one last look in its mirror at her deficient proboscis.

She snapped the compact shut and tossed it on her desk. She then inhaled deeply, lowered her chin, and strode purposefully toward the supply room door. Grasping the knob, she forcefully wrenched open the door and saw Dr. Septum examining Nurse Spray's . . .

8.14 PORK ROLE

The ability to synthesize apparently unrelated bits of information to produce something new is an important aspect of creative functioning. This exercise will help stretch your ability to produce original ideas and integrate them into meaningful patterns.

Assume that you are a writer for a magazine that features short stories. Your job has been to take story titles suggested by your boss and develop an appropriate narrative to fit. Recently you have been so successful that your boss has become a little envious. So she decides she will test your creative powers by giving you the following line: "When the string is long, the pig is short."

Using this statement, write a brief story that will be appropriate for the title.

8.15 NOVA SPEAK

Most languages continually evolve. We coin words which eventually are added to everyday speech. This ongoing process of inventing new words increases the richness of language. It also provides new meanings and ways to express ourselves.

As a basic exercise in originality, invent meanings for the following nonsense words:

Flimmelfrod
Primundant
Smetverian
Braxvolterod
Gindeooper

8.16 CREATE THAT EXERCISE

For your "final exam" in originality, make up your own exercises for improving different aspects of creative thinking. Try to develop at least two exercises for Chapters 4 through 10.

COMMENTS AND SAMPLE ANSWERS

8.02 FILL OUT

8.03 DRAW-A-WORD

Here are some sample drawings for the words. Yours might be completely different, which is OK since there are no right or wrong answers to this exercise.

CA$H

RADIO

TELEPHONE

ELEVATORS

The letter arrived by AIRMAIL on M T W TH F S S. It offers the first LOOK at the administration's 1 P 2 R 3 I 4 O 5 R 6 I 7 T 8 I 9 E 10 S as the UNIVERSITY prepares to TRIM its budget needs to MEET expected LE VELS of FUNDING.

8.04 PICTURE THAT

Automobiles

Telephones

Computers

Bicycles

Tanks

8.05 SOMETHING NEW

Electric Can Opener

1. Cutting disk	Make it reversible
2. Clamp	Make it wider, make it conform to the hand
3. Motor housing	Eliminate ridges to make it easier to clean
4. Magnet	Make it removable for cleaning

Blender

1. Container	Make it unbreakable
2. Blade	Thicken it or use stronger metal
3. Base	Widen it or add suction cups to bottom
4. Push buttons	Use a dial instead

Toaster

1. Heating elements	Make them movable to obtain desired degree of darkness
2. Lever	Eliminate; toast automatically enters toaster
3. Darkness control	Adapt to adjust distance of heating elements from the toast
4. Housing	Make it transparent

8.06 GRID LOCK

Using a chair as the object, the following attributes might be selected:

wood	multipurpose
plastic	wide
long	soft
round	comes apart
light	electrical
tall	many colors
movable	

With these attributes, a chair could be designed that has a wooden frame, uses molded or pliable plastic for the seat, is relatively long, has rounded edges, is light in weight, is designed especially for tall people, can be moved easily, has several different purposes, is extra wide, is soft to sit in, is disassembled easily, has electrical devices to serve its various functions, and comes in a variety of colors. For instance, the chair might be moved electrically to different sitting positions, instantly mold to the sitter's body (something like a bean-bag chair), double as a seat for a car or as a lawn chair, vibrate, dispense drinks, etc.

8.07 LABEL IT

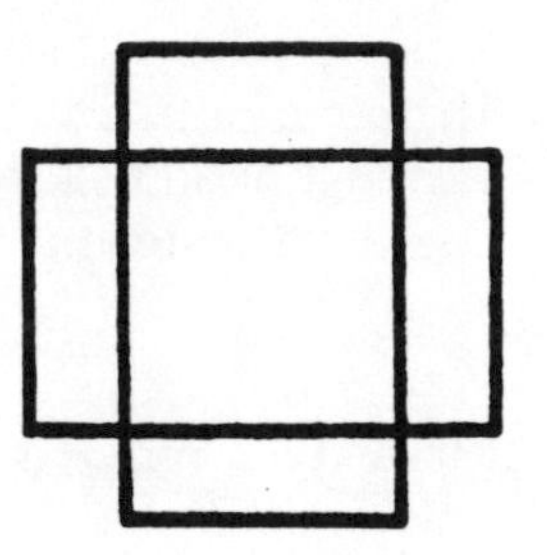

1. Backtangle – from the "backs" of four rectangles

2. Boxrim – from the top edge of a square box

3. Di-arrow – two arrows joined together at their base

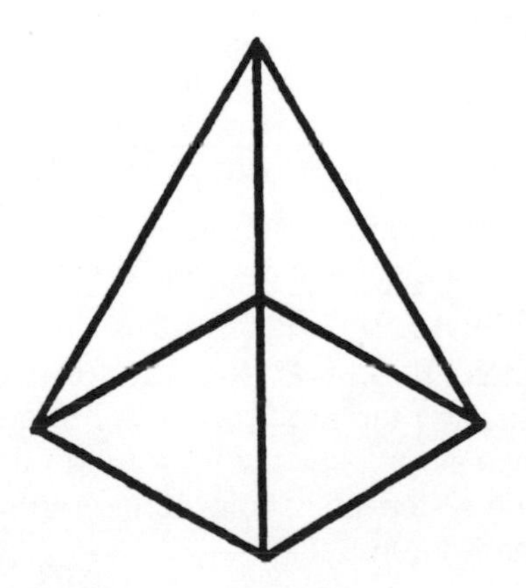

4. Pyrabase – from the base of a four-sided pyramid

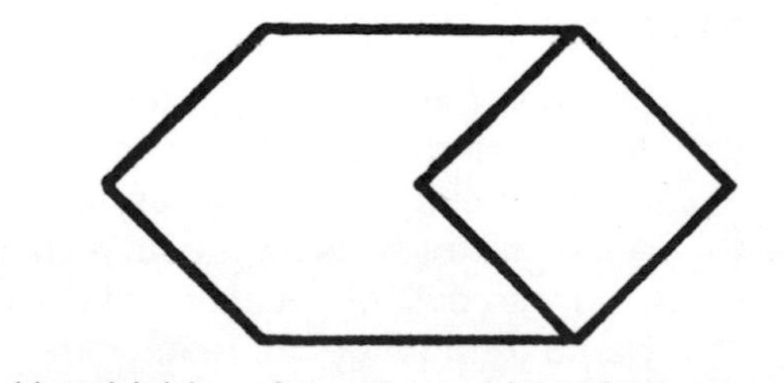

5. Hexabiside – from two sides of a hexagon

8.08 LIGHT UP YOUR LIFE

One way to prompt ideas for this exercise is first to make a list of all the relevant characteristics of a light bulb – bulb-shaped, glass, screw action, uses electricity, replaceable, vacuum inside, filament element, breakable, bright, easily turned on and off, emits light beams, glows, etc. Such a list is also likely to help you break away from any constraints you might impose on yourself about a light bulb and, consequently, will result in more creative solutions. A few possible solutions for each object are:

bookcase: sliding glass doors, lighted shelves, electrically opened doors, easily broken down and reassembled, vacuum to keep dust out.

mailbox: transparent to see mail, lights up when mail arrives, doubles as a lamp post, spring to automatically reclose mailbox door, box unscrews from post to stop delivery.

calculator: screws into a pen, glows in the dark, can be used to activate other electrical devices, disposable calculators, projects data onto a wall screen.

broom: handle unscrews for easy storage, doubles as a flashlight, shaking the broom makes it glow so it can be used as a toy space sword, shine light through bristles for sweeping in dark corners, top of handle screws into a fixture for easy hanging when not in use.

lawn mower: vacuum pickup of grass clippings, inexpensive, replaceable blade, transparent gas tank to tell when empty, filament line to replace blade, light for dawn and dusk mowing, filament track underground to guide mowing, automatically turns off when it hits a solid object.

8.09 WORD TO WORD

Bit-Ply	Plywood formed into parquet patterns.
Rat-Tulip	A new breed of tulip that "eats" household flies.
Brat-Lip	A pliable cup lip for children to teethe on.
Tab-Tip	A tab pull for soda cans with a tip that is convenient to pull, eliminating injured fingernails.
At-Pit	Name for a barbecue restaurant.
It-Plum	New fruit dessert.

Rib-Put	Device to secure injured ribs.
Bat-My	New children's baseball game that can be played by one child alone.
Bib-Mill	A bib to collect grounds from a coffee mill.
Bait-Pill	New bait form for fishing.
Bra-Pull	A quick-release brassiere.

8.10 NAME THAT EXERCISE

• Chapter 3

Current Name	Possible New Name
Triadic Deeds	Bragging Rights
On Purpose	Your Bent

• Chapter 4

Current Name	Possible New Name
Goal Visualization	Seeing Ahead
How Much Are You Worth?	Dollars and Sense
Think About It	Creative Living
Early Bird	Rise to the Occasion
Imagine That	Picture Yourself
Bunny Hop	Splitting Hares
Problem Detective	Creative Divorce
Quadruple D	All in the Family
Nitty Gritty	Getting to It
What Problem?	Look It Over
Good Sense Shopping	Eye Shopping
Visual Smorgasbord	Strange Thoughts
Mind Mapping	Brain Patterns
Name That Letter	Alphabet Hunt
Disfigured	Figure Misfit

• Chapter 5

Current Name	Possible New Names
Your Room	Know Your Space
The Picnic	Eating Out
Touch It	In a Bag
I Hear Ya	Sound It Out

Sensory Stretch	Out to Sense
Be a Banana	Dining With the Monkeys
Mowing Along	Can You Cut It?
Goodness Sakes	A Positive Eye
Cube Imagery	Shape Sorter
Orange Elephant	Color Me Orange
Brain Vacation	Tripping Out
Thoughtful Images	Imaginary Thoughts
Working Out	Pleasant Dreams
Goodness Sakes II	Thinking Good Thoughts
Square Search	Squared
Tabloid Attention	Don't Touch Me!
Plane to See	Flying to See You

- Chapter 6

Current Name	**Possible New Name**
Square Off	Lines Galore
Don't Fence Me In	Hold Off
Create a Viewpoint	Silly Patterns
Switch Around	Rotating Dots
Symbol Relatives	What Is That?
Spy Telegrams	Secret Messages
Breakdown	Tear It Apart
Take a Stand	Look But Don't Touch
Take It Off	A Jug of Wine and . . .
Just Like That	Almost the Same
SDRAWKCAB	Turnaround
Would You Believe?	Stretch 'n' Solve
Fantasyland	Daydreams
Silly Inventions	Make It Weird
Just Suppose	Design a House
Cut-up	Pie in Your Eye
Fill 'er Up	Neatnik?
Dots the Way	Shapely Shapes
Letter Line-up	Up and Down Letters
Paper Waltz	Sheet Walking
Strip Tease	A Tearing Experience

- Chapter 7

Current Name	Possible New Name
Brain Gusher	Mind Poppers
Pre-fix It	But First . . .
Letter Hunt	Lost Letters
Underweight	Taking It Lightly
Word Chains	Linking Words
Sniff Out	Bottle It
Word Relatives	Something Like It
Gar-báge	Stinking Ideas
Go to Class	Grouping Around
Don't Forget	Try to Recall
Column Relatives	Force It
Just Alike, Only Different	Common Grounds
It Came From Beneath the Blot	Blot It Out
What's In a Name	Bureaucrat's Delight
Spy Stories	Storyteller
It Takes Two	Word Duals
Alphabet Associations	Association Relations
Funny Knife	Died Laughing

- Chapter 8

Current Name	Possible New Name
Steaming Ideas	What's Bugging You?
Fill Out	Sketch It
Draw-a-Word	Picture Words
Picture That	Sign In
Something New	Break and Change
Grid Lock	Pick an Object, Any Object
Label It	Call It Like It Is
Light Up Your Life	An Illuminating Idea
Word to Word	Backward Inventing
Name That Exercise	Call It Something
The Master	A Crumbling Experience
End It All	Long John Shiver
Nasal Nonsense	A Nose by Any Other Name
Pork Role	Pig Out
Create an Exercise	Starting Over
Nova Speak	May I Have a Word?

• Chapter 9

Current Name	Possible New Name
Values	It's Worth It
Wired Up	A Wiry Choice
Light the Way	Lamp of Your Life
Category Crunch	Groupies
Weigh In	Car Trouble
Criteria Cafeteria	Raising Your Standards

• Chapter 10

Current Name	Possible New Name
Idea Garden	Dig It
Freeze-Unfreeze	Cold Shoulder
Consultant	Thanks, Uncle Harry
You Can Take This Job and . . .	Take Charge
I Scream	Never on Sundae

8.11 THE MASTER

One possible interpretation involves the "chain of life" concept. Small bugs eat crumbs, the small bugs are eaten by bigger bugs, which in turn are eaten by small animals, which are eaten by larger animals, which then are eaten by humans. At the interpersonal or societal levels, the chain of life could be a metaphor for how we all are dependent on one another in some way. Thus, our potential to meet the needs of each other could be viewed as part of the purpose of our existence.

8.12 END IT ALL

For inside the room he saw eight burly-looking men standing around one slender, frightened man who was completely naked. But what was most distinctive about the naked man was the way he appeared to be shivering. His knees were flapping together but his upper body didn't seem to be cold at all.

Quickly scanning the scene, Greg's eyes caught hold of what he feared most. Over in one corner, neatly hung on a polished wooden hanger, was a pair of white long johns – for the legs only. From the way they were swinging freely on the hanger, Greg surmised they just had been removed from the man. It was then he knew. Yes, this is it – the lair of the dreaded Long John Dons, notorious for their savage acts of forced long-john removal in the coldest of weather!

8.13 NASAL NONSENSE

. . . and saw Dr. Septum examining Nurse Spray's nose. They hadn't heard her enter yet, so she was able to overhear a portion of their conversation. From what she could gather, Dr. Septum was fitting Sally for a new nose.

"That feels pretty good, doctor," Sally said as the doctor adjusted the artificial nose over her own. "Now I'll have a nose just as big as Dr. Snaffle's."

Cora was flabbergasted. She interrupted their conversation and, although startled, they agreed to let Cora examine Sally's new nose. Cora was so impressed that she asked Dr. Septum to fit her with one. Dr. Septum reached into his nose bag and pulled one out, placing it carefully on Cora's nose. At that very moment Cora realized that here was the answer to her problem – right over her very own nose!

8.14 PORK ROLE

Hog production can be a confusing business, to say the least. In addition to the need for tolerance of continual squealing, there must be an efficient way of processing large numbers of these creatures. One major problem is separating the large from the small pigs for processing. Although it is easy to tell the very large from the very small pig, only a trained porkologist can decide about pigs of moderate size, since regulations require either a large or small size classification.

One company solved this problem by hiring Professor Porcine to advise them. The professor said that the simple solution is often the best. His suggestion was for porkologists to tie a long string to the tail of every small pig, so that when the pigs went to processing, the processors could easily make the necessary distinction.

8.15 NOVA SPEAK

Flim-mel-frod: 1. One who deceives others. **2.** a long pole used to prod Flimmels (Med. Eng.)

Pri-mun-dant: The state or quality of being primund. **1.** species superiority. **2.** a very boring animal; a repetitious animal, most notably vertabrates which repeat themselves.

Smet-ver-ian: One who attends to Smets. At one time, someone who ate only Smets. This practice was outlawed in 1923.

Brax-volte-rod: Ancient Norse sport similar to modern day pole vaulting. Participants used metal rods and performed only during lightning storms. From May 1 of 443 A.D. until May 2 of 443 A.D., Braxvolterodding was the most popular sport of its time. Interest waned due to a lack of participants.

Gindeooper: The sound made while eating a jumbo hotdog with sauerkraut. [Archaic: A very clumsy alcoholic from Holland.]

8.16 CREATE THAT EXERCISE

If you turned to this page expecting to see fourteen more exercises, you'll be disappointed. Do you think I can make up exercises forever?!!! You're the one who's supposed to do the work this time!

All seriousness aside, you may gain more from doing this exercise than from most of the others combined. By developing material instead of reacting to it, your understanding of basic creative-thinking principles should increase immensely. There's really no substitute for doing. In addition, this exercise required you to use both sides of your brain . . . something we all need a little more practice doing.

When you've finished all of your exercises, rate yourself on your own originality. Use a seven-point scale to describe each of your exercises as being not very original (1) to very original (7). Then figure out why you rated the exercises the way you did. If you didn't rate yourself very high, it may be because you have unrealistic expectations. The exercises in this book probably are no better or worse than your own. You are unique and you shouldn't expect to do everything like the rest of us. If you rated your exercises very high in originality, you probably should be writing your own book instead of wasting your time reading this one. Or perhaps you have expanded the powers of your creative mind from just doing the other exercises in this book. In either event, it would be time to pat your right brain for a job well done.

If you are especially pleased with any of your exercises, I would be interested in seeing them. Just send them to me in care of the publisher (Bearly Limited, 149 York Street, Buffalo, NY 14213). If I ever do another edition of this book I may be able to include some of them in it. You, of course, will be given full credit. I won't be able to return any, so make yourself an extra copy if you wish.

9

You're The Judge

Making decisions is my second most favorite thing to do. My most favorite is trying to flush my head down a toilet.

I really don't like to make decisions. It's much easier to hope a problem goes away and solves itself, or to let someone else do the dirty work. I would prefer to delegate my decisions to a special Personal Decision-Making Committee. By the time THEY get around to making a decision, the problem will have disappeared.

Unfortunately for me and for others with similar feelings, we must make decisions, some for our very survival. So we might as well learn to do the best we can.

In creative problem solving, decision making is one area we frequently overlook. Creativity is not limited to generating ideas. We also have to narrow the ideas down and decide upon a workable solution.

For the exercises in this chapter, you will need to relax your creative mind a bit and switch over somewhat to the analytical mode. Don't completely abandon your right brain, however. You'll need it to generate selection criteria, and evaluate the factors and values that will influence your final decision.

The exercises are designed to help you accomplish the following things:

1. increase your awareness of values so you are more satisfied with your decisions;
2. consider values in comparison to general factors;
3. narrow down and combine ideas to make a final choice easier;
4. increase awareness of the criteria you use in decision-making;
5. increase your ability to make choices from equally-attractive alternatives.

9.01 VALUES

The importance of values in decision-making can't be minimized. They affect the way we perceive problems and guide us in making choices. If we increase our awareness of our values, we might be more satisfied with the outcomes of our decisions.

For this exercise, identify which values guided you in making some important decisions in the past (a career choice, having children). Select one of these major decisions and list at least ten values that influenced your choice. Then rank the values in terms of how much influence they had on your final decision.

One example could be that of an engaged woman who really wasn't sure if she wanted to be married. The values that guided her decision not to marry may have been listed like this:

1. CAREER ADVANCEMENT: I couldn't just pick up and move to a new city if my career demanded it.
2. FINANCIAL INDEPENDENCE: I would have to account to someone else for the money I spend.
3. FREEDOM OF CHOICE: My vacation plans would have to be guided by someone else's preference.
4. SOCIAL ACTIVITIES: My free time would be restricted by having to get home to cook dinner.
5. EMOTIONAL TIES: I would daily have to be attuned to the moods of another person.
6. IMPULSIVE ACTIVITIES: I couldn't exercise in the living room during prime time TV programs.
7. CLEANLINESS: My house wouldn't be as neat as it is by living alone.
8. CONVENIENCE: Someone else would be using the bathroom in the morning.
9. DIET: I couldn't eat salad every night for dinner if I was tempted by pizza.
10. IT'S *YOUR* MESS: I'd be angry if I didn't get help in household tasks I now do myself.

The next time you have an important decision to make, list your values and rank them as you did for this exercise. See if you can use the ranking to help you make your choice. Then, sometime after you have decided, assess your satisfaction with the decision.

9.02 WIRED UP

Assume you are the president of a corporation that manufactures wire coat hangers. Business being good, you decide to seek new uses for your product.

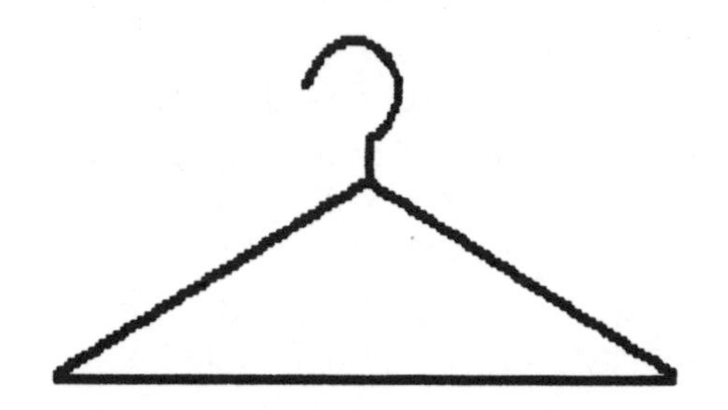

A brainstorming session with your staff generates these ideas.

1. Key rings
2. Puzzle games
3. Picture hangers
4. Hole punchers
5. Cooking grills
6. Small bird and animal cages
7. Trellis for climbing plants
8. Christmas wreaths
9. Letters for signs
10. Mousetraps

Your task is to select five items for serious consideration as new product lines. When you make your choices, write down the factors that influenced you and pay particular attention to WHY they influenced you.

Regardless of which products you selected, you were influenced by factors specific to you as well as others more general. For example, specific to your product might be the fact that sharp bends in the hanger could crack the paint. Therefore, you may not have chosen letters for signs.

More general factors would be ease of assembly, cost, or the likely market. The reasons why you were influenced by any of these factors is a comment about your values as well as your knowledge.

9.03 LIGHT THE WAY

It often is difficult to decide when there are several alternatives from which to choose. Furthermore, each person will vary considerably in the factors they use to make a decision.

This exercise will help you assess how you approach decision-making when you are confronted with four different alternatives. To benefit the most, consider all factors that influence your choice. Write down each factor as you become aware of it, being as specific as possible.

Which design for a table lamp (Figure 9.1) do you like the best, and which the least?

In making your judgments, you might have begun with style preferences for, say, traditional over antique. Your reasons for such preferences are difficult to determine, but many of us are influenced by our experiences. For example, what person might have influenced you to prefer traditional to antique?

In evaluating your experience with this exercise, consider these questions:

1. Do your likes and dislikes fall into similar categories?
2. How did you process the information you used for your choice?
3. Did you use a sequential or a skipping around procedure?
4. Were you more affected by overall appearance? by a particular shape?

Figure 9.1 Proposed designs for a tablelamp.

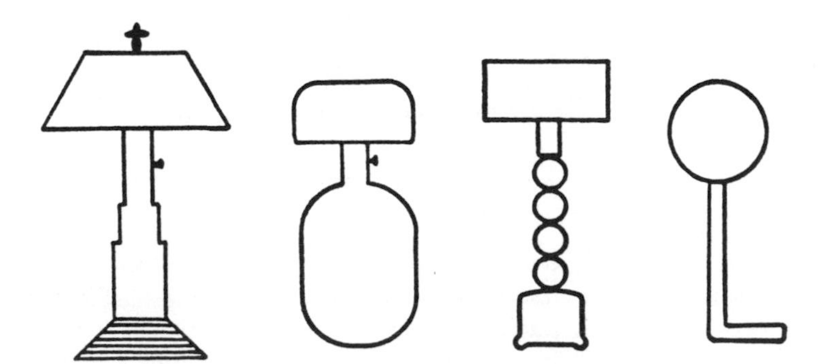

When answering these questions, ask yourself why you thought the way you did. Problem answers are just as important as awareness as to why you make the decisions you do.

9.04 CATEGORY CRUNCH

Decisions are especially difficult when you are presented with alternatives you find equally attractive. One way out of this dilemma is to combine and modify several ideas to produce one or two final solutions. This is done by clustering similar ideas into categories, and then modifying or combining several ideas within the categories to produce one workable idea. You can do this successively until only three or four categories remain.

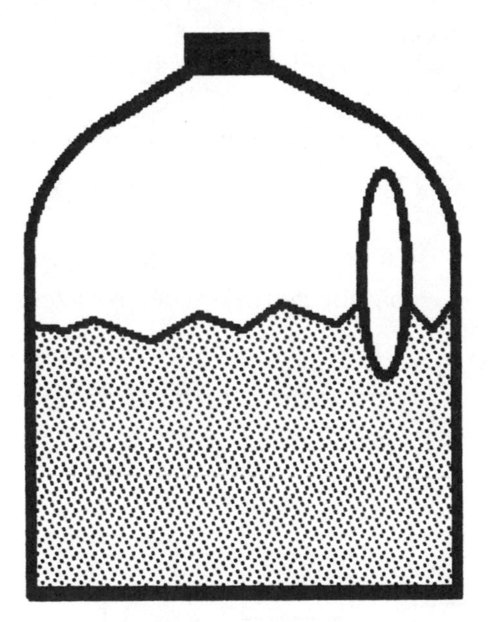

Suppose, for example, you had these ideas as ways to use a one-gallon plastic milk container.

1. funnel
2. flowerpot
3. storage for emergency water supply
4. disposing of used engine oil
5. party hat
6. bird feeder
7. flotation buoy
8. packaging material
9. toy for children
10. small-parts storage

These uses could be categorized as a container (2, 3, 4, 6, 10); as a functional device other than a container (1, 7, 8); as a decorative item (5, 9). The three categories then could be reduced to just two: containers or functional devices, and decorative items.

The number of items could be reduced further by combining items within categories. A funnel and small-parts storage might suggest a funnel device for holding screws.

Combine and modify the following solutions for a problem on how to obtain funds for a nonprofit preschool. (Suggestions for categories are publications, media, manufacturing, services, soliciting, and one-time activities.)

1. have a telethon
2. have an auction
3. start a magazine
4. get company sponsors
5. solicit contributions from the wealthy
6. have a fund-raising carnival
7. free babysitting in exchange for professional fund-raising services
8. have children collect donations door-to-door
9. have a concert
10. seek a federal grant
11. write a book
12. have a bake sale
13. take care of pets for a fee
14. make and sell ice cream
15. get a university film department to produce a film
16. get funds from rich relatives
17. make and sell toys
18. get free public service announcements from radio and TV
19. publish a newsletter
20. have a raffle

9.05 CRITERIA CAFETERIA

Criteria are standards that help us make decisions. The quality of our decisions often is affected by how many criteria we use and our awareness of them. Always think of as many criteria as possible and then select the most relevant to you. Remember, be specific, for that makes criteria easier to judge.

List as many criteria as you can for the following decision situations.

1. Buying a house
2. Buying a car
3. Renting a video cassette
4. Buying a pair of shoes

Rank the criteria from highest to lowest in importance TO YOU. Example number three might be listed thus:

Likely entertainment value, cost, length of rental period, compatibility with VCR, preferences of others who might view it with you, distance of store from home.

Be aware that the criteria ranking will vary according to your personal needs and preferences or for different situations. For instance, someone who lives three hours from the nearest video store would rank length of rental period and distance from home as most important. If you own both a Beta and a VHS system, compatibility would not matter.

9.06 WEIGH IN

When we make decisions about everyday affairs, most of us use simple guidelines to help us choose. "Product A costs less than B; therefore, I will buy A." When we make such decisions, however, we may be unaware of other factors we unconsciously considered, or we may not pay much attention to them.

Sometimes a more structured, systematic procedure is more useful in developing higher-quality decisions. When a decision is an important one, a systematic approach can make the difference between success and failure.

This exercise provides practice in choosing from three high-cost alternatives. It is classified as high-cost because of the financial commitment to the decision-makers.

You have spent the entire day searching for a replacement to your six-year-old station wagon, the same car that failed to start on the morning your wife was about to give birth to your youngest son.

The same car that decided to take a vacation in the airport parking lot when you returned from yours.

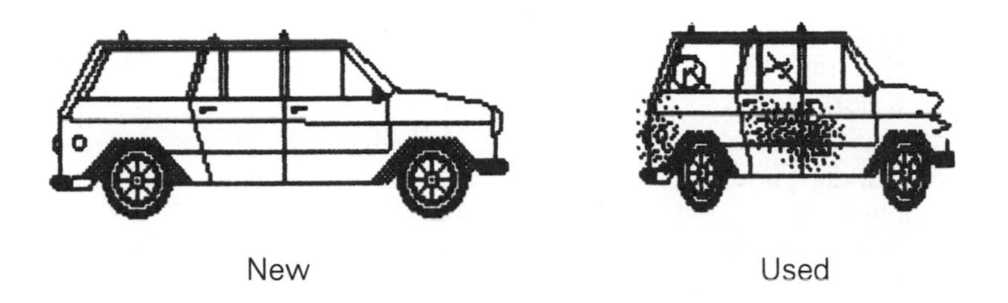

New Used

The boys are now screaming and your wife's back hurts. Luckily you have narrowed your choice to three cars. Make your choice using the following procedure:

1. List the factors that will influence your decision.
2. Rate each factor from 1-5 in its importance to you (1 = not very important).
3. Think of three cars you actually would consider buying.
4. Rate each car (1 = not at all) as to how it would meet the importance standards you established in Step 2. This is the satisfaction rating.
5. Multiply each importance rating times each satisfaction rating for the three cars.
6. For each car, add up the products obtained from multiplying and make your decision.

If you have trouble following these directions, study the example shown in Table 9.2 on page 148. Then develop your own decision chart.

Even after going through all the steps, you may decide you don't want to abide by the final outcome. Your gut instinct may be to go with car C. If so, rethink the ratings; are there any you would change? any you would omit?

A common error is to reject the final rating without being aware of why you did so. Reviewing the factor list and ratings can help ensure this error does not occur.

Figure 9.2 Decision chart for selecting a car.

Satisfaction	Importance	Car A		Car B		Car C	
1. Price	5	3	15	5	25	1	5
2. Gas mileage	5	4	20	3	15	2	10
3. Color	3	5	15	1	3	5	15
4. Dealer service	4	4	16	5	20	5	20
5. Handling and comfort	4	4	16	3	12	5	20
6. Repair record	5	4	20	5	25	4	20
7. Seating capacity	5	3	15	2	10	5	25
8. Ease of servicing	3	5	15	2	6	3	9
9. Trade-in value	2	5	10	2	4	3	6
10. Styling	4	5	20	3	12	5	20
			162		132		150

Based on the final ratings, car A would be selected over cars B and C.

10

Avoiding Surprises

You know Murphy's Law: If anything can go wrong, it will. Remember the times you dropped your toast on the floor, jelly side down, right into the mud the dog just tracked in? Or when you took that trip and remembered to bring the toothbrush you usually forget? Now . . . where did you put the toothpaste?

Although we may try to anticipate potential problems, we're not always successful. Unplanned events always seem to develop at the last minute. And the more complex the project, the more numerous and complicated are the things that can go wrong.

A perfect example is the first launching of the space shuttle. The computer malfunction that occurred in the final stages of countdown could have been avoided. But humans were involved, and we haven't reached the stage of perfection that allows us to avoid mistakes. (Although we probably all know one or two individuals who would have us believe otherwise about themselves!)

The world's best ideas are without value unless their end result has a chance for success. Sometimes we try so hard to solve a problem without thinking it through first. It's a human trait to want to start right in on the project.

The young teenage musician who wants to be a rock guitarist perhaps thinks he can pick up the instrument and play complicated riffs on his first try. But did he reckon with the need to first develop blisters, then callouses, on his fingers? Did he take into consideration the tedium of the hours of practice required to build dexterity?

The housewife who's an accomplished seamstress decides to sew her own drapes for the living room. "The drapes won't be a problem," she thinks with the utmost confidence. But the finished drapes have an unattractive sag in the middle of the rod, and the nails are pulling free of the wall. She realizes she didn't plan for the weakness of the plaster around the window and she didn't coordinate the weight of the fabric with the strength of the curtain rod.

Planning and anticipation of possible problems are sometimes neglected in the creative problem solving process because it can be difficult to give them the attention they deserve.

Motivation doesn't come from a book, it can't be purchased in a store. We need to practice using some exercises and methods designed to emphasize the importance of planning and anticipating.

The exercises in this chapter will help you with important elements of creative problem solving:

- Develop a creative climate to gain acceptance of your ideas.
- Evaluate your persuasive and analytical powers.
- Assess your personal strengths relevant to implementing ideas.
- Anticipate potential implementation problems.
- Develop an implementation planning diagram.

Most importantly, these exercises force you to fully use both sides of your brain. To do otherwise at this point in the process would be unproductive.

If you're too analytical, you could overlook potential problems and creative ways to overcome them. Too creative and you'd have trouble developing the systematic procedure that allows your ideas to reach fruition. You need to integrate the funtioning of both your brain hemispheres.

10.01 IDEA GARDEN

You can become so involved in contemplating the potential problems of implementing your idea that you overlook the importance of developing the right creative climate. The environment has to be receptive to your idea. So you must consider what, if anything, needs changing before you can put your idea to work.

A garden can't be planted without soil preparation: you need to determine if the soil contains the proper nutrients for what you desire to plant; plow the earth to break down resistance to the seedlings; add fertilizer, plant the seeds and water regularly.

Using the analogy of a garden, these are the steps you might take to develop the creative climate to ask your boss for a raise.

1. Decide what to plant. — What are your strengths and weak-

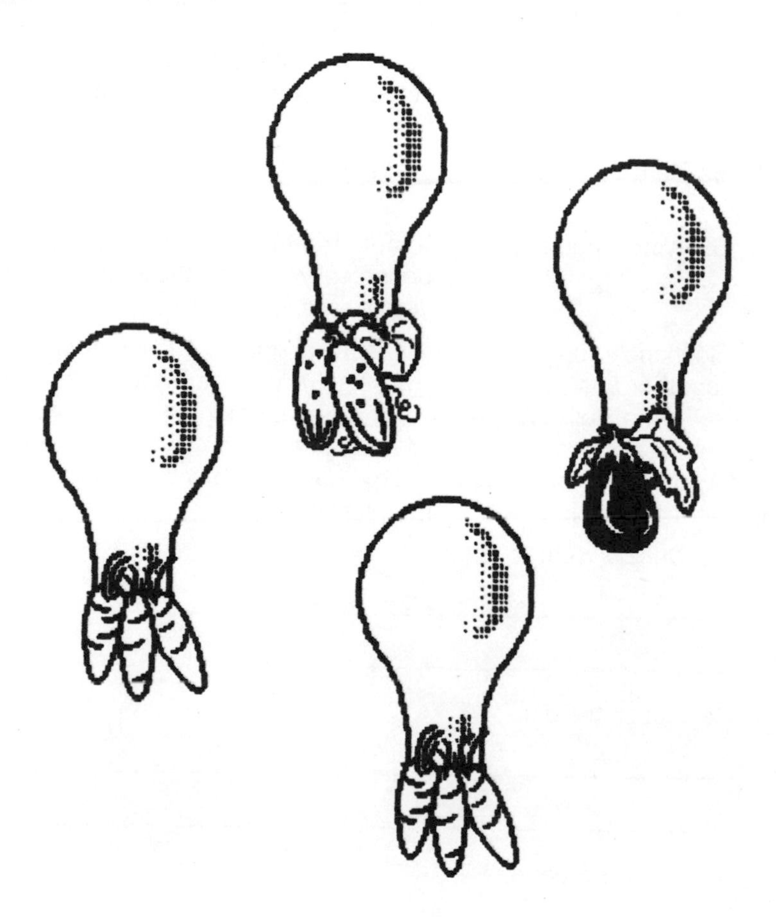

	nesses? Which needs to be emphasized?
2. Check the soil.	How receptive is your boss to employees asking for raises? What approach is likely to produce the most favorable response? Which times is your boss in the best mood?
3. Plow the earth.	Is your boss receptive when you discuss your work performance and point out the contributions you have made?

4. Add fertilizer.	Have co-workers or other persons in authority mention your qualifications to your boss.
5. Plant the seeds.	Mention that you think you deserve a raise.
6. Water regularly.	If not immediately given the raise, periodically mention the subject to your boss.

Scenario: Your direct supervisor has just left the company to take another position. You're aware that management plans to advertise in the Help Wanted ads for a replacement. You believe you could step into the job with little difficulty.

Again using the garden analogy, how would you convince management to consider you for the position?

1. Decide what to plant.

____

____

2. Check the soil.

____

____

3. Plow the earth.

____

____

4. Add fertilizer.

____

____

5. Plant the seeds.

____

____

6. Water regularly.

10.02 FREEZE - UNFREEZE

The value of your creative idea can't be measured until it is accepted by those who eventually will use it. Look at the area of new product development. Only a small percentage of proposed ideas actually reach the commercialization stage. Acceptance is needed anytime someone tries to persuade another about the merits of an idea.

The key to gaining acceptance for your idea usually lies with your persuasive powers, or those of the people who will put it into action. You'll have more control over the persuasion process if you take time to anticipate your customer's possible objections and analyze the likely benefits. What factors will be judged in assessing the worth of your idea?

Assume you're involved in marketing a new product called Frig-I-Door, curtains of heavy clear-plastic strips that are hung, using Velcro fasteners, across supermarket frozen-food cases to keep cold air in and hot air out. Customers make their selections by reaching between the strips. A four-foot section of the curtains costs about ninety dollars.

What are the primary benefits of Frig-I-Door that will make it attractive to supermarket officials?

1. Decreased energy costs.
2. Cooler temperatures mean longer shelf life.
3. Hot weather shutdowns will be minimized.
4. Adjacent aisles are kept warmer, thus making shopping more comfortable for the shopper, especially in winter.
5. Easy to clean.
6. Possibly lower costs to the consumer due to reduced energy costs.

What objections might the potential buyer have to the product and how could you counter their concerns?

1. Initial cost. A 36-foot section on a case costs about $800.	Research has shown energy costs will drop 20-30%, offsetting the initial investment in a short period of time.
2. Appearance detracts from attractive food display.	Will be partially offset by increased customer comfort during cold weather and perhaps lower food costs.
3. Strips would make reshelving difficult.	Velcro fasteners make it easy to peel away the screens to restock food items.

In addition, a trial period could be offered. If energy costs are not substantially reduced, the product could be returned for a partial refund.

Scenario: You are in a position to implement new training programs within your company. You believe that if all employees attended an intensive four-hour course on the fundamentals of delivering quality customer service, the result would be positive for the company's reputation and profitability. You plan to have training start at the uppermost levels of management and waterfall down through the organization.

Using the Frig-I-Door outline as an example, describe what benefits the training program would achieve, possible objections you might receive, and countering comments.

Benefits

____

____

____

____

____

____

____

Objections	Countering Comments

10.03 YOU CAN TAKE THIS JOB AND . . .

Okay. That's the last time you're going to sit and take it while your boss reams you out for not doing things his way. You've had it and decide to quit. You feel a lot better but . . . what now? Aha! Become your own boss and you would never have to put up with that kind of stuff again. You'll make your own hours and the sky is the limit concerning how much money you can earn. So why not? Go ahead and start planning. But remember: you also like to eat and have a house to live in.

Use these questions as guidelines:

1. What are your major strengths and skills?
2. Which one could you turn into a profitable service or business? Why?
3. What will be the name of your business?
4. Where will your facility be located or will you operate out of your home?
5. How much initial capital will you need?
6. How many employees should you hire and what will be the organizational structure of your business?
7. Who will be your market and how will you reach them?
8. Who is your competition?
9. What will your advertising brochure look like?

Now, apply some negative creativity or reverse brainstorming. Make a list of all possible factors that could go wrong. For example, suppose you decide to develop a mail-order business to sell gold-plated toothpicks. An example of a negative-creativity list for your mail order business is shown here.

Potential Problems	Preventive Actions	Contingency Plans
1. Wood in short supply	Substitute plastic	Raise prices
2. Gold in short supply	Substitute silver	Raise prices; use gold paint
3. Cost of wood too high	Raise prices	Substitute plastic
4. Cost of gold too high	Raise prices	Sell conventional toothpicks.
5. Not enough customers	Offer discounts	Hire ad agency
6. Toothpicks break when first used	Use quality control	
7. Competition too tough	Lower prices	Use deluxe packaging; aim for exclusive buyers.
8. Cost of factory space too high	Begin production at home	
9. No workers interested in working for you	Offer profit sharing	Use relatives

Of course, such a chart is only as good as the information it contains. If you're not thorough, you could develop a sense of false security. You must continually review your chart to make sure you haven't left anything out.

Scenario: You have decided to leave your company and begin

your own consulting business. Produce your own planning list by answering the nine questions on page 155.

1. ______________________________
2. ______________________________
3. ______________________________
4. ______________________________
5. ______________________________
6. ______________________________
7. ______________________________
8. ______________________________
9. ______________________________

Once you're satisfied there are no omissions or required changes, develop a negative-creativity list, using as a guideline the mail-order business list shown previously. For every potential problem, write a preventive action to counter each negative consequence. For the ones that could put you out of business, develop a back-up or contingency plan.

Potential Problems	Preventive Actions	Contingency Plans
________	________	________
________	________	________
________	________	________
________	________	________
________	________	________
________	________	________
________	________	________
________	________	________

Potential Problems	Preventive Actions	Contingency Plans
______	______	______
______	______	______
______	______	______
______	______	______
______	______	______
______	______	______
______	______	______
______	______	______
______	______	______

After you've created your lists, go back over your original plan to see if you need to change anything.

Now, go do something else for at least an hour.

Okay, now that you're back, review your entire plan. Can you find something you overlooked the first time? If so, you're making sure you won't receive an unexpected or disastrous surprise.

10.04 I SCREAM

Most of our activities are based on some sort of plan. It can be one that is carefully thought out in advance or put into action relying on past experience alone. Familiar activities require little planning. However, when we need to implement a new activity, especially one that's important, it's necessary to develop a plan.

The plans we create can be extremely simple or complex. They can range from a brief checklist of things to do to a highly complex flow chart that needs to be monitored by a computer. In between these two extremes lies a method known as planning diagrams.

These are relatively simple flow charts that show what needs to be done and how to do it. The core of a planning diagram consists of various decision points used to guide all subsequent actions. It's really just a network of activities and decisions. However, a certain skill is required to determine what activities to include and how to relate them.

To illustrate, consider the task of constructing an ice cream sundae made of vanilla ice cream, chocolate syrup, and nuts. It's to be eaten from a bowl with a spoon.

Figure 10.1 Planning diagram for an ice cream sundae.

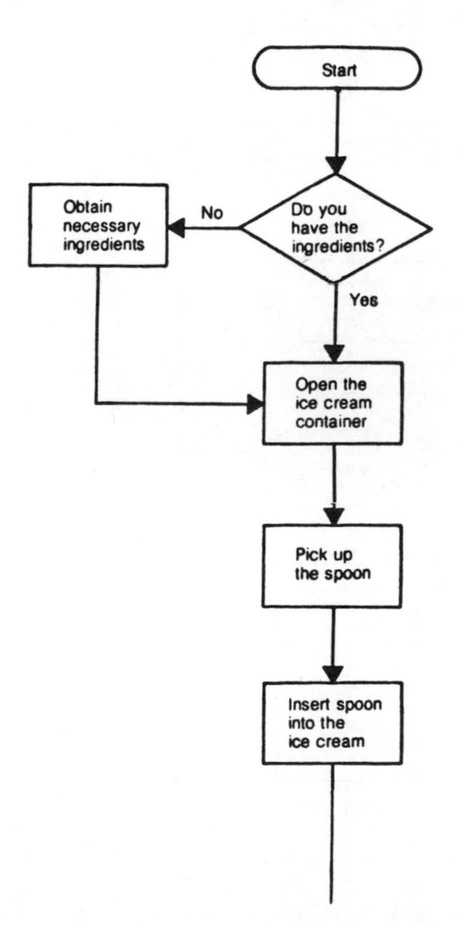

Figure 10.1 Continued.

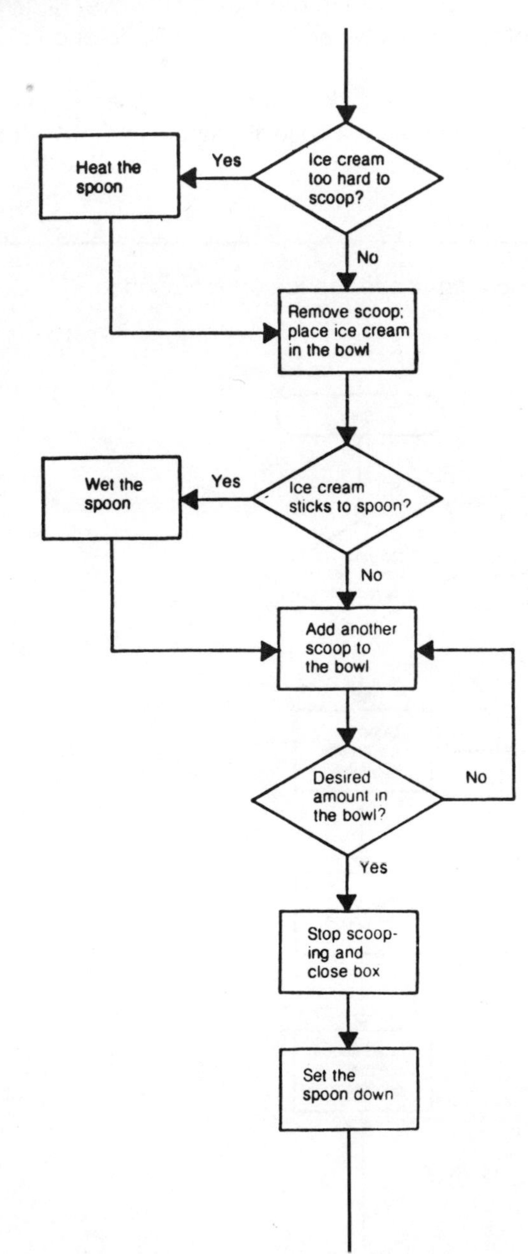

Figure 10.1 Continued.

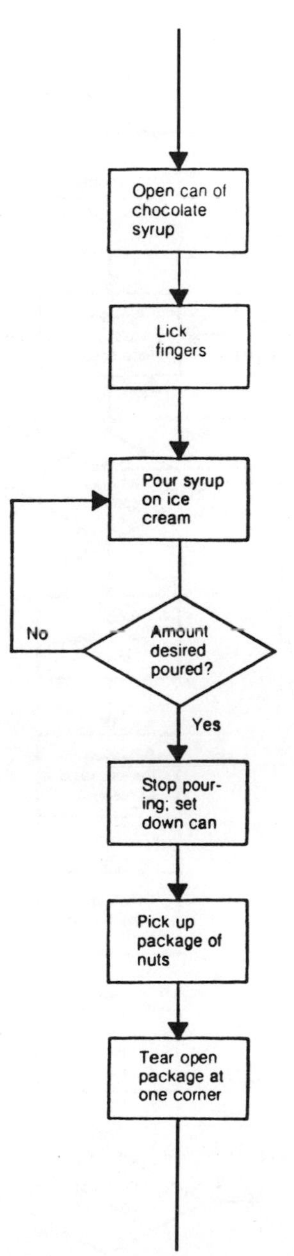

Figure 10.1 Continued.

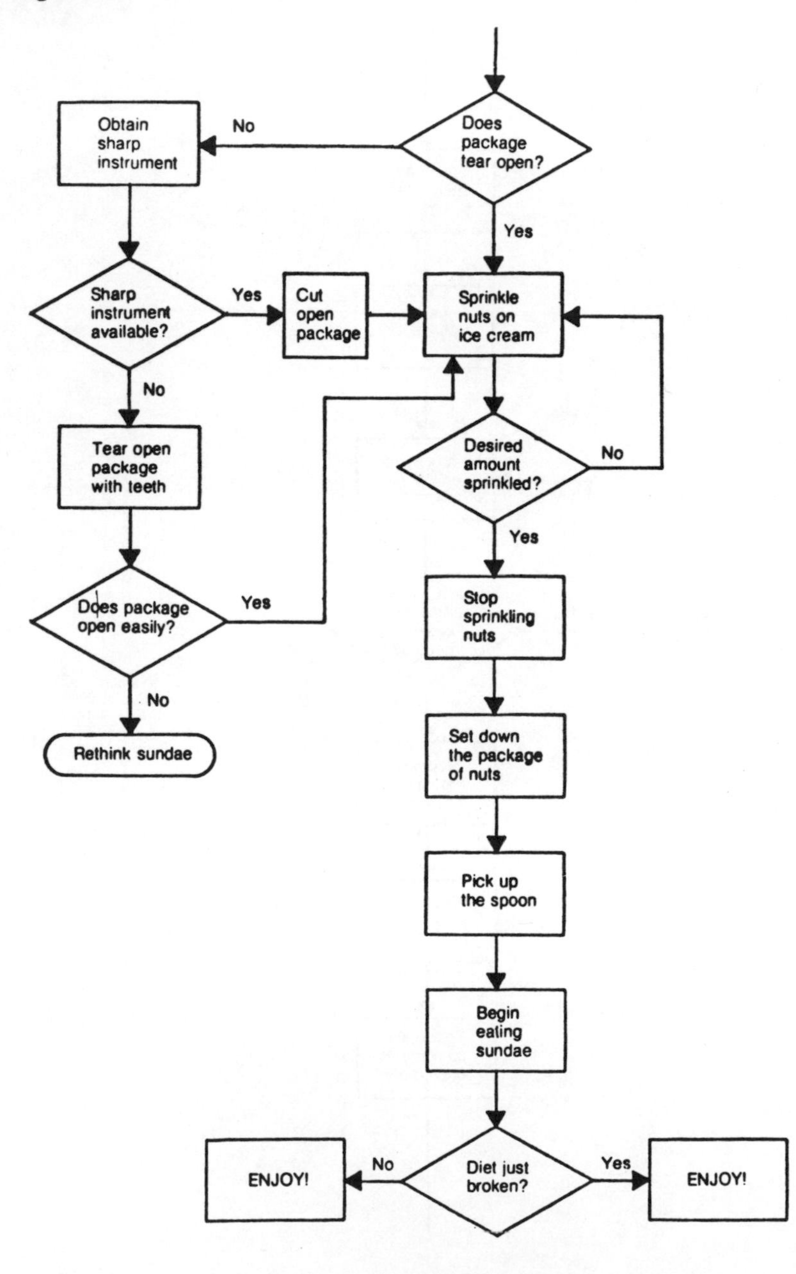

When making a planning diagram, it's better to include too much detail rather than too little. Planning diagrams can make the difference between implementation success or failure in important projects.

Construct your own planning diagram that will record the steps you would take to create a proposal for the quality-service training program mentioned earlier. Include everything involved from writing the program proposal and getting it approved, to producing hard copies and delivering the training.

11

Applying The Exercises

By now you have completed the warm-up and intermediate phases of your program at least once. Unless you feel the need to repeat any of the exercises, you can begin the applied phase.

This phase is designed to help you further internalize some of the major creative-thinking and problem-solving concepts, and to help you seek closure to your program. It is important that you pull together all the conscious and even unconscious experiences and learnings you have gone through up to this point. Unless you can make right-brain thinking a part of your natural thinking processes, you will find your left brain regaining control. And the best way to internalize your new skills is to apply what you have learned.

The third phase of your program involves two sets of applied activities. The first presents you with a hypothetical problem to work, using your learning from the previous phases. This is to get you thinking about how right-brain processes help you solve the problem presented. The second activity is similar, except that it is a personal problem of your own choosing. You have "ownership" of this problem, and thus your motivation to solve it should be much greater than in the case of the first problem.

By being motivated, your problem-solving skills are heightened so that the overall experience will have more meaning and will be retained or internalized more than had you worked on a problem with little meaning to you. One of your ultimate objectives in completing this program should be to become a better creative thinker. And you can't expect to be a creative thinker unless you are able to think creatively just as routinely as you think analytically.

USING A PROBLEM-SOLVING PROCESS

It should now be clear to you that a major emphasis throughout this book has been on creative thinking as a tool for problem solving, particularly unstructured problems – those which have no clear-cut solutions. Besides personal growth benefits you might reap from becoming more creative, the primary benefit to you will be to help you become a more effective problem solver. If you think more creatively, you can approach unstructured problems with more confidence and with a greater probability of solving them.

To become a more effective problem solver requires some knowledge of the basic problem-solving process.

Problem solving generally is discussed in a strictly left-brain manner. A linear model is presented and then described in terms of the sequential activities required to proceed through each of the stages. Because most people are used to such a left-brained presentation, it can't be criticized in that respect. There has to be some way of communicating information about processes, and a sequential approach to problem solving is one with which most people probably can relate easily.

I have intentionally avoided presenting a problem-solving model at the beginning of this book even though it has been a recurrent theme throughout. Although problem solving is integrally related to creative thinking, the emphasis in this book on right-brain thinking led me to defer discussing problem solving until you had progressed through the exercises.

Since the exercises themselves were organized roughly into major problem-solving stages, my hope was that you would learn about many of the activities involved in the creative problem-solving process as you experienced the exercises. For example, when you were doing the exercises in Chapter 4, you were practicing problem preparation and gathering facts about yourself and problems; in Chapter 5 you were experiencing awareness of your different senses and how they can aid you in analyzing problems and generating ideas; in Chapters 6, 7, and 8 you were practicing some of the skills needed to generate ideas: flexibility, fluency, and originality; in Chapter 9 you were looking at how you might evaluate and select ideas; and in Chapter 10 you were practicing gaining acceptance for your ideas and anticipating idea-implementation problems.

All these activities are involved, in one form or another, with the creative problem-solving process. An example of this process can be depicted as shown in figure 11.1, which is fairly typical in the nature of activities included. Note that it also is a prescriptive model rather than a descriptive model. That is, it shows what *should* occur during the process and not what actually *does* occur.

The process begins with identification of a problem situation. This is followed by a search for information about the problem to help clarify it. Using this information, a definition of the problem is developed and used as the basis for generating possible solutions. This stage is critical to the entire process since the initial definition will determine the nature of most subsequent activities. After possible solutions have been generated, they must be evaluated, using criteria that conform to any constraints on the problem, and a solution (or solutions) must be selected. Actions then are taken to gain acceptance for the solution – to smooth the way for its implementation. Finally, the solution is implemented and followed up and monitored in the last stage to insure that it will achieve its objectives.

In Figure 11.1, various feedback loops signify that adjustments may be needed during the course of the process. For instance, new information might become available during the selection stage that could alter the selection of one solution over another. And, after a solution has been implemented, it may create new problems that could necessitate beginning the process over again. Note that this model is essentially a closed-loop model.

All of this is very rational and logical. The model implies that the different stages are relatively clearcut and, if followed correctly, will lead to a successful solution. However, most of us seldom use such a model to solve our problems. There are situations in which muddling through can be just as effective. Nevertheless, whenever there are high costs associated with not solving a problem, we would be wise to adopt a more systematic approach.

The approach we adopt, need not be as structured as that shown in Figure 11.1. The approach should be one we can conceptualize easily and with which we can identify easily. We need to start thinking of the creative problem-solving process in terms of our own right brains. How can we personally visualize this set of ongoing activities that will take us from a problem "mess" to some sort of satisfactory solution?

My personal attempt at such a visualization is shown in Figure 11.2. To me, this type of conceptualization is more logical than the standard model. The numbers represent the same activities shown in Figure 11.1, but in this case there is no prescribed sequence. In fact, several different solution paths are represented in the figure.

After being confronted with the initial mess, you might proceed

Figure 11.1 Example of a standard Creative Problem-Solving Process.

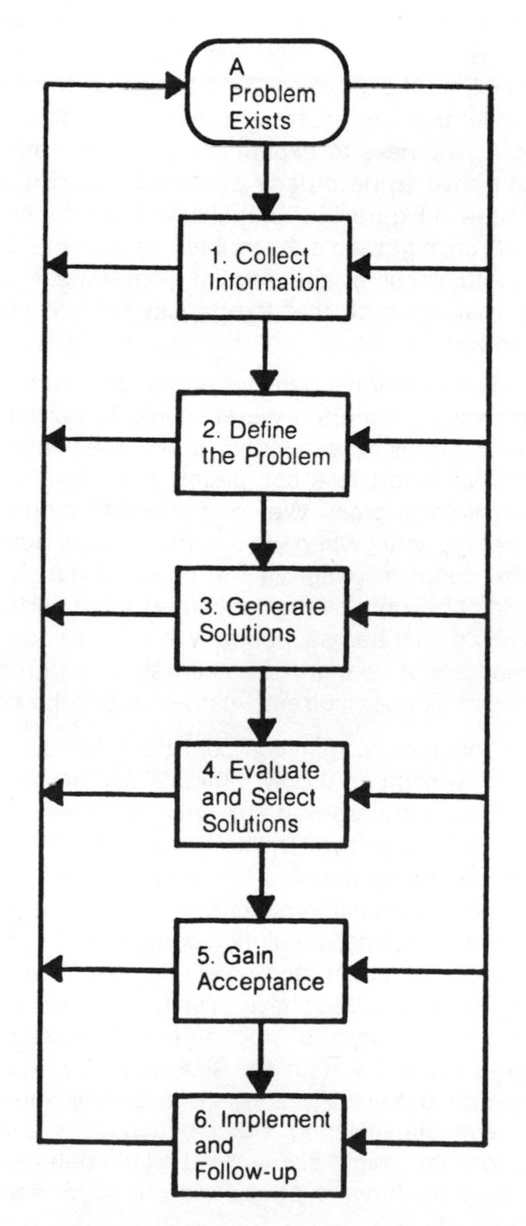

in any direction, since the numbers represent points in undefined space. The direction followed will be based on intuition and logic. You could proceed in a linear fashion or skip from one stage to another. This is not to say, however, that there is or should be complete chaos to the process. Some type of format has to be followed in order to make progress toward the goal of resolving the problem mess. You have to experience some forward movement, but it doesn't have to be orderly or strictly sequential. Thus, the path you choose in Figure 11.2 probably will vary for each problem. Also note that you might solve the problem at any time. The outcome doesn't have to occur at the end of some linear process. Circumstances may be such that things just fall into place and the problem is solved.

This is what usually happens when we deal with unstructured problems. However, too often we succumb to our left brains and try to maintain a logical, sequential procedure. Then, when this method fails, we revert to a completely right-brain approach, but end up making little progress. We need to capitalize on the strengths of both our hemispheres when we use the creative problem-solving approach. We need to recognize the need for different activities, but we shouldn't become overly concerned about performing these activities in any prescribed sequence. We need to be more holistic and concerned about relationships than about whether a specific set of activities has been correctly carried out at the correct time.

To apply this type of thinking, consider what approach will be best for you in working on the hypothetical and personal problems. In order to retain some consistency with the presentation format of the exercises, I suggest you think in terms of the following general stages: 1) problem preparation and information collecting, 2) problem awareness and definition development, 3) testing problem assumptions and constraints, 4) solution generation, 5) solution refinement, 6) solution evaluation and selection, and 7) implementation planning. Of course, you don't have to be locked into these particular stages. Feel free to vary the procedure as long as you seem to make progress toward a solution. At a minimum, try to separate your efforts into broad stages of: 1) analyzing the problem, 2) generating ideas, 3) evaluating and selecting ideas, and 4) planning implementation. You might skip around a little between these four areas, but strive for forward progression through them. You need

Figure 11.2 Example of a modified Creative Problem-Solving Process.

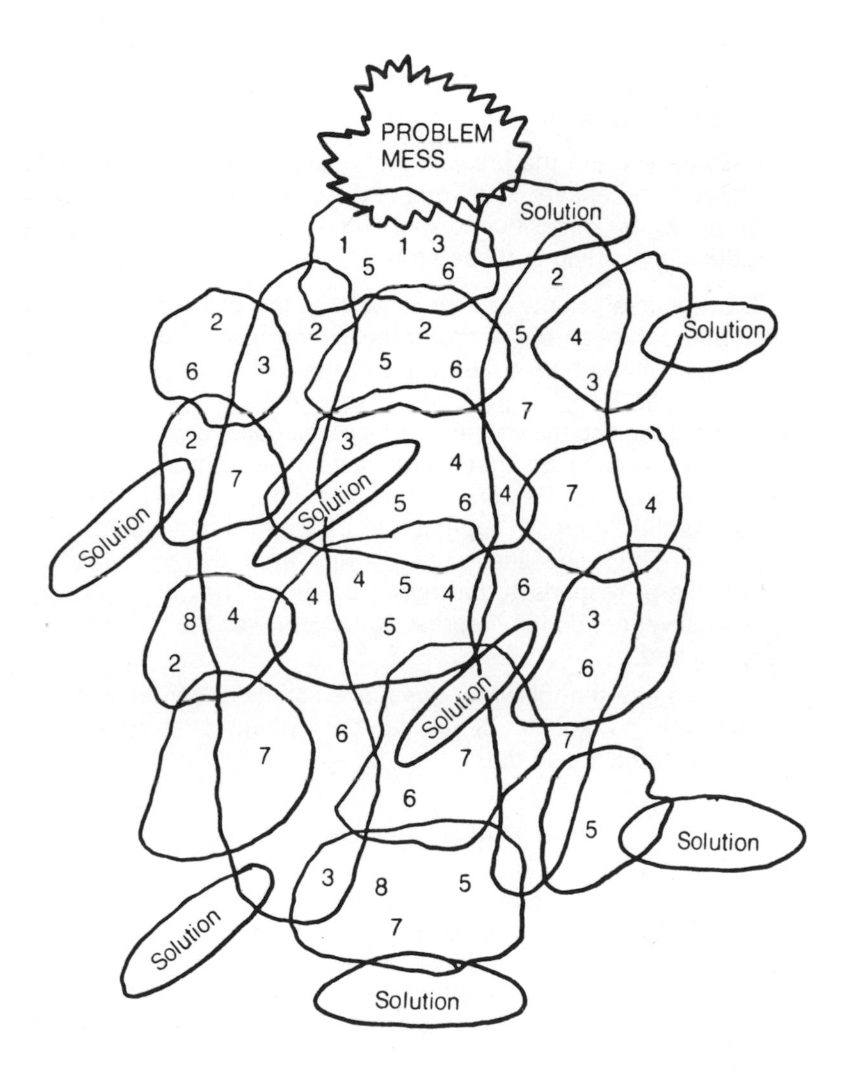

some degree of goal orientation, even though it may be slightly fuzzy at the outset.

PROBLEM NUMBER ONE

Here's the hypothetical problem for you to use in applying your learnings from the exercises:

> Assume you are the president of a large chain of department stores. In recent years, several of the stores have been plagued by increasing losses due to shoplifting. In what ways might you reduce shoplifting in these stores?

Allow yourself plenty of time to work on this problem. After you have worked through the entire process, compare your responses with the partially worked-out example at the end of the chapter. You might find that some of the sample responses will suggest new ways of approaching the problem or new solutions. If you are stimulated by the example, go ahead and make any changes you wish to your own responses. Be careful, however, that you don't use the example as the "correct" approach or as your primary standard of comparison. The responses in the example are only representative of the types of responses that might be used. They definitely are not exhaustive, nor do they represent the only way the problem can be approached.

You can use the following questions as guides for helping you work through the problem. If you can think of any other considerations, go ahead and use them.

1. Getting Ready
   a. How do you personally feel about this problem?
   b. What do you know about shoplifting?
   c. Can you develop mental images of someone shoplifting?
   d. What would stores be like if there were no shoplifting?
   e. What information do you need to solve this problem?
   f. How might you go about collecting this information?
   g. What are the major, essential characteristics of the problem?
   h. Which characteristics of the problem are related?
   i. Which characteristics of the problem are more important than others?
   j. Who shoplifts?

k. What do shoplifters steal?
l. Where do people shoplift?
m. When do people shoplift?
n. Why do people shoplift?

2. What's happening?
   a. Can you tune in to the problem to describe in sufficient detail what you would see, hear, touch, taste, or smell in shoplifting situations?
   b. Can you vicariously experience the thoughts and feelings of a shoplifter at the moment of taking something?
   c. What's good about shoplifting? In what ways might shoplifting benefit stores and/or other people?
   d. Can you imagine the awareness levels of shoplifters, store employees, and customers in the store while a shoplifting act is occurring? How much do they see and hear at this time?
   e. What different types of noises, lights, voices, etc. might attract or deter shoplifters?
   f. How would you define the problem at this point?

3. Loosening Up Your Mind
   a. What are the constraints of this problem?
   b. What assumptions do most people make about shoplifters and shoplifting?
   c. Can you challenge any of these assumptions? How?
   d. What cultural taboos might help shoplifters?
   e. What elements of shoplifting are similar to one another? What elements are different?
   f. What else is like shoplifting?
   g. What reversals can you think of to describe the shoplifting problem?
   h. How can you exaggerate the objectives of a shoplifting reduction program?
   i. What fantasy solutions to the problem can you develop?
   j. What is the silliest possible solution? What practical solution can you develop from this?
   k. Look over all your responses. In what ways might you redefine the problem now?

4. Letting Go
   a. How many different solutions can you think of in ten minutes?

b. For the moment, forget about the shoplifting problem. In five minutes, how many different ways can you think of to prevent people from doing something? Do any of these ideas suggest possible solutions to the shoplifting problem?
c. Select five different objects from your immediate environment. Give yourself three minutes to consider each object. How many different solutions can you think of that might be suggested by the objects?
d. Look over your list of solutions. Can you combine any to produce new solutions?

5. Being Different
a. What makes you mad about shoplifting? In what ways might you change these factors to develop problem solutions?
b. What new names can you think of to describe your solutions to this point? Do these names suggest new solutions?
c. Can you use the different characteristics of a light bulb to suggest possible solutions?
d. Write a brief, one- or two-paragraph story about shoplifting. Make it silly, if you wish. What new ideas are suggested by this exercise?
e. What is different about your solutions?
f. Can you think of any improvements that could be made on previously tried solutions?

6. You're the Judge
a. What values are relevant to shoplifting incidents?
b. Can you reduce the total number of solutions you have generated to three to five categories? Can you combine any of these solutions?
c. What criteria will your solutions have to satisfy in order to solve the problem?
d. How important are each of these criteria relative to the others?
e. Can you construct a rating chart to help you narrow down your choice of solutions?
f. Which solutions would be most likely to solve the problem?

7. Avoiding Surprises
a. Are there any obstacles to implementation that would be

difficult to overcome?

b. What are the worst possible things that could go wrong with your solution?

c. How likely is it that each thing could go wrong; how likely is it that each problem could be prevented?

d. How serious would be the consequences if each thing anticipated went wrong?

e. What might be done to prevent these things from happening?

f. What specific steps will you need to take to implement your solution?

g. What people will have to be persuaded about the worth of your solution?

h. What are the major benefits of your solution?

i. What additional resources will you need for implementation?

j. What new problems are likely to be created by your solution?

k. How could others be rewarded to help you with implementation?

l. What will you need to do to follow up implementation of your solution?

PROBLEM NUMBER TWO

The second problem should be a personal one you have wanted to resolve, but haven't had the time; or a problem you have been actively working on, but with little success. Select a problem you feel you must solve to reduce some tension within yourself.

Use the same questions or modified versions as guides that you used for the shoplifting problem. Be flexible in your approach. Defer all judgment until you are ready to select a solution, and maintain forward motion during the entire process. Also allow plenty of time to work on this one.

After you have selected one or two possible solutions and have made plans for implementation, try to implement your solution. If you were working on a problem of some significance to yourself, approach it with the expectation you can and will solve it. Unless you actually take the final step of putting your solution to work, you will have just gone through the motions in training your mind. Your brain needs feedback, and actually solving a problem is one of the best ways to get this feedback. In doing so, you will help yourself to grow further as a creative person – and you should find the experience to be pleasurable as well. There's a lot of truth to the old saying that nothing succeeds like success. So think positively and solve your problem. I know you can do it.

SAMPLE RESPONSES TO THE SHOPLIFTING PROBLEM

Note: The following is presented in a sequential, left-brain manner only to communicate the information more easily. When I actually worked through the problem, I found myself skipping around quite a bit. However, this disjointed activity will not be too apparent from the description.

1. Getting Ready

   a. I feel very upset that people steal merchandise, since the costs are passed on to the consumer, and that some people think they have the "right" to shoplift because of high prices. On the other hand, I feel sorry for poor people who only take clothes for their children.

   b. People shoplift because they are poor, to see if they can get away with it, for the fun of it, because of peer pressure, or because of severe psychological disturbances. Some people have developed elaborate devices (coats with pockets sewn on the inside) to aid them; they generally are considered to be professional shoplifters. For other people, the act of shoplifting is more spontaneous. Both employees and customers are guilty of shoplifting. The problem is extremely costly to both stores and customers. Many stores have taken special precautions to thwart shoplifters (e.g., electronic devices).

   c. I can see someone casually walk through a store, look around, slip a small item into a pocket, and walk out of the store.

   d. Expensive merchandise would be displayed more openly; there would be no security measures; prices would be lower; store personnel would observe customers less closely.

   e. If what I think I know about shoplifting is fact or opinion; how many people in a store at a given time are likely to shoplift something; the type of merchandise stolen most frequently; the type of person most likely to be a shoplifter; the time of day and day of week most shoplifting occurs; the reasons most people shoplift, etc.

f. Discussions with store personnel, consultants, journals, and academic publications.

g. The conditions most likely to tempt someone to shoplift; motives; areas of stores that are most susceptible, etc.

h. Perhaps age of shoplifters and time of day (e.g., teenagers after school hours). Would need to do more research to answer this question.

i. Again, I would need to do more research to answer this question.

j. Teenagers, blue-collar workers, white-collar workers, housewives, people from all economic levels.

k. Coats, sweaters, pants, shirts, blouses, rings, necklaces, tools, etc.

l. In all store departments except furniture and large appliances.

m. At all times of the day; when they think they can get away with it.

n. To save money; to punish themselves; to prove something to someone else; to get back at someone else, etc.

2. What's Happening?

a. I see a lot of people walking around and examining merchandise. There are many different types and sizes of people and a variety of different colors worn by each. I see a lot of glass, metal, and carpeting in the store. There is a constant level of talking, sounds of clothes hangers, and necklaces being placed on glass countertops. The glass is very smooth in places, but sticky in other places from constant touching. My feet walk smoothly over the well-worn carpet. I am surrounded by smells of perfume, body odor, leather, and food in a bakery shop.

b. The clerk has just turned his head so I probably could slip this tie inside my coat. He just looked in my direction, so I'd better be very careful. Maybe if I just turn my back toward him just a little. There. Now I'll check on the clerk one more time. He's busy now, so . . . oops, here comes another customer, but he's more interested in the suits. OK, here goes. I'll just pick it up and quickly stuff it in my coat pocket. I won't even look around while I'm doing it. Now, to just casually walk away from here and out of the store. It sure feels good to have gotten away with that. Why did I do that?

c. One positive feature about shoplifting is that it provides a way for some people to obtain merchandise they couldn't otherwise afford. It also may be a form of psychological release for some people. Other people might benefit from shoplifting by a feeling of social well-being if they deter a shoplifter or report one to store management; it provides an opportunity for people to do a good deed. Stores might benefit from good customer relations by showing customers that management is concerned about the problem and doesn't want to raise prices unnecessarily.

d. Most customers probably aren't aware that shoplifting is going on unless they happen to observe it directly and the act is very blatant. The shoplifters themselves will be very tuned in to their environment, pick up many visual and auditory cues that other customers might miss. Store employees are likely to be very aware of the actions of customers, especially those who act suspiciously.

e. A lot of loud talking and low lights probably would be attractive to shoplifters.

f. In what ways might shoplifting by customers be reduced? In what ways might store personnel be more aware of potential shoplifters?

3. Loosening Up Your Mind

a. A major constraint might be to view a solution as requiring that shoplifters be caught in the act. Another constraint might be to view all shoplifters as alike.

b. Most people may view shoplifters as belonging to the lower economic classes; most people may view shoplifting as not being a major problem.

c. I already have challenged these assumptions when I analyzed the problem along other dimensions. I would, however, need to gather data to substantiate my claims.

d. Two taboos would be minding one's own business and

not getting involved. Such attitudes might make it easier to shoplift.

e. Some similar elements would be the need of all shoplifters to avoid being caught, and the fact that most store personnel are trained to watch out for people who may shoplift. Different elements would include such factors as the time of occurrence, the type of merchandise, and the type of shoplifter.

f. Shop-lifting is like:
   (1) taxes – the consumer always pays a price.
   (2) a packrat – higher consumer prices are exchanged for stolen merchandise.
   (3) stealing books from a library.
   (4) cutting grass – the problem can be eliminated temporarily, but always returns.

g. In what ways might customer shoplifting be increased? In what ways might customers be motivated to give merchandise to the stores? In what ways might shoplifters develop a need to turn themselves in?

h.

Original objective	Stretched objective	Possible solutions
easy to implement	difficult to implement	frisk all customers as they leave the store.
increase profits	decrease profits	give discounts to customers reporting shoplifters.
maintain good customer relations	alienate customers	use qualifying standards to enter the store; start a buying club.

i.

Fantasy solution	Practical solution
Read the minds of all customers.	Develop psychological profiles of shoplifters.
Shoplifted merchandise becomes invisible when taken from store.	Use an exploding dye that is triggered when certain items are removed from a display rack.

A force field prevents shoplifters from entering the store.	Require all coats and packages to be left at the door before entering the store.

j. Ask all customers to please not steal anything. A practical solution would be to develop educational programs in the schools and the local news media.

k. In what ways might:
(1) customers be screened before entering a store?
(2) poor people pay for clothes?
(3) shoplifters be less aware of the store environment?
(4) merchandise be displayed to reduce shoplifting?
(5) subliminal messages be used to discourage shoplifting?
(6) store clerks be trained better to detect shoplifting?
(7) customers help reduce shoplifting?
(8) sounds, lights, textures, colors, or temperature deter shoplifters?
(9) the public be educated better about the shoplifting problem?
(10) more shoplifters be caught in the act?
(11) shoplifters be encouraged to return stolen merchandise?
(12) all customers be frisked before leaving a store?

(Note: All of these redefinitions of the problem actually are subproblems that can be used to suggest possible solutions. The major problem is still preventing the occurrence of shoplifting. However, these problem redefinitions help provide a new perspective on the problem. Any one or all of the redefinitions could be selected to use in generating numerous other solutions.)

4. Letting Go
a. Offer incentives to return stolen merchandise, establish a bartering unit in each store, increase the number of security personnel, use electronic detection devices, put all merchandise in display cases and order by number, have subliminal messages put in store music, offer discounts to customers reporting shoplifters, convert the store into a buying club with qualifying standards for acceptance, put an electrical field

around merchandise that will set off an alarm if tripped, convert to catalog sales, install visible cameras to scan areas of frequent shoplifting, offer free counseling to shoplifters who turn themselves in, stage mock arrests of store employees acting like shoplifters, and have a monthly "shoplifter's day" in which the arrest records of prior shoplifters are made known.

b. Put up a wall, ask them not to do it, physically restrain them, drug them, find out what is rewarding to them and reward them when they don't do it, subject them to peer pressure, lock them in a room, immobilize them, electrically shock them if they try to do it, sit on them, tie them up, educate them with the pros and cons involved, glue them down, make a rule, confuse them, and charge them too much money. From these ideas might come such practical solutions as only allowing people to view merchandise without touching it, offering customer discounts if shoplifting is reduced within a certain time period after they have attended an educational program, paying customers to report shoplifters, and selling only very large, expensive types of merchandise.

c. I have selected a glass, a stapler, a telephone, a plant, and a clock. Glass: Put merchandise in display cases, require customers to ask to see merchandise (like asking for a glass of water), use a one-way mirror on the ceiling from which store personnel can watch customers. Stapler: Put merchandise in boxes which require pushing down on a lever to open. Whenever a lever is pushed down, a light shows on a TV-monitored control station so the customer can be observed inspecting the merchandise, or staple tags to merchandise that must be neutralized electronically before leaving the store. Otherwise, an alarm will sound. Telephone: Call in to the store to place orders, then pick up at the store; give customers a constantly changing code number that must be dialed before opening a display case or picking up merchandise to inspect it; pick up merchandise in a store by using a telephone receiver connected to a voice-stress analyzer. Anyone whose voice indicates a high stress level must contact a store clerk for assistance. Plant: Sell only expensive merchandise that customers are not allowed to examine without a clerk; use a photoelectric beam which, if broken, sets off an alarm; or have merchandise rigged so that sound vibrations of it being moved outside of the store set off an alarm. Clock: Use a timing device that sets off an alarm hidden in the merchandise unless it is turned off before picking up the object; hypnotize all shoplifters, using a ticking sound, so they'll never steal again.

d. Some of the solutions could be combined as follows: Customers apply for a combination credit card and security card that is used to unlock the store, record who has entered, unlock display cases (recording the card number), and make purchases. Another solution would be to offer discounts to customers who attend educational programs on shoplifting.

5. Being Different

a. Shoplifting makes me mad because I have to pay higher prices, I have to put up with security devices and suspicious sales personnel, and because some people think they are entitled to steal due to past injustices done to them. Solutions from this "bug" list might include distributing the price increases due to shoplifting among the shoplifters who are caught, and designing a store in which all potential customers would volunteer to undergo a security check so they would not be bothered by security precautions while in the store.

b. Some possible labels for different solutions would be: Catch-a-Crook; Shopping for Shoplifters (customers turning in shoplifters); The Trading Center, Swap It (for a bartering department); Big Brother (for store cameras); Crooked Sounds (for voice-stress analyzer); Your Time is Up (for timed alarm system); Buy-Safe, You're OK (for credit/security card). No new solutions are suggested to me by these labels.

c. Possible solutions from characteristics of a light bulb include:

(1) screw-action: secure small appliances with screws; have merchandise rotate in a controlled-access display case.

(2) breakable, emits light: to inspect expensive items, a light beam is broken, notifying store personnel.

(3) easily turned on and off: a store clerk turns a switch to permit opening a display case for customer inspection of the merchandise inside.

(4) filament element: tie down merchandise with a nylon line.

d. It's not easy being a shoplifter. Society looks down on you; you're constantly looking over your shoulder. It's especially awkward at cocktail parties when someone introduces you as their friend the shoplifter. You get very little respect.

If more people realized what was involved in becoming a truly competent shoplifter, perhaps more respect would be given to this elite corps. Considerable planning and organizational skills are needed to pull off a successful "lift" – skills that probably rival those of most business executives. An ability to get along with and relate to other people is essential as well. You must be capable of talking your way out of many difficult situations, and it's always nice if you can relate well to your fellow prisoners and the police. The art of shoplifting has been neglected for too long now, and it is time that more recognition is given to this growing profession. Perhaps what is needed most is development of a professional organization complete with its own public relations department. That and an efficient bail-bonding system would go a long way toward upgrading the profession.

Possible solutions suggested by this story are: publication of shoplifter arrest records, formation of a local merchants' committee to combat the problem, and "shock" programs in which first-time shoplifters would visit the local jails and talk with police about the consequences of their actions.

e. Although I am not acquainted with all the measures that have been taken to combat shoplifting, I would guess that some of my solutions are different in the following ways: (1) involving other customers to stem the problem, (2) emphasizing rewards for not shoplifting instead of punishment for doing it, (3) restricting access to a considerable variety of merchandise, and (4) the notion of a bartering unit to soften the urge to take something from a store.

f. Many of my proposed solutions are modifications of previous solution attempts or solutions currently in practice. For example, many stores keep small, very expensive items in display cases. Some of the solutions use the display-case concept, but vary in the way access is gained to the cases.

6. You're the Judge

a. The act of shoplifting, its effect on other people, and the shoplifters themselves may reflect such values as justice, equality, self-esteem, security, power, dignity, and honesty. Any decision as to the best solution should incorporate many of these or similar values.

b. The 43 solutions generated in the previous stages are presented in Figure 11.3. Using the numbers of these solutions, I have organized them into five categories, as shown in Figure 11.4 (two of the solutions are listed twice, since they overlap into one other category). Among the solutions that could be combined easily would be solutions: 1 and 22; 4 and 8; 18 and 34; 2, 3, 35, and 37; 13, 27, and 32; 14, 15, 24, 26, 28, 29, 31, 33, 35, 38, 39, 40, and 41; 9, 19, 20, 21, 36, 42, and 43.

c. Major criteria might include the cost of the effort, its likelihood of success, ease of implementation, effect on customer relations, time required, effect on sales, and extent to which major physical changes in the store would be required.

d. The criteria could be ranked from highest to lowest importance as follows:

(1) likelihood of success
(2) effect on sales
(3) cost
(4) effect on customer relations
(5) time required
(6) physical changes required
(7) ease of implementation

e. To illustrate construction of this chart, a one- to five-point rating scale is used to evaluate the five solution categories described in Figure 11.4. (For more information on how to construct such a chart, review the Weigh-In exercise.)

f. Based on these ratings, the solutions in the customer-involvement category (I) would be most likely to solve the problem, while educational efforts (Category V) would be least likely to stem the incidence of shoplifting. As constructed, this chart represents a shortcut to the overall evaluation process. To be more thorough, the solution combinations within each category should be subjected to the same procedure.

Figure 11.3 List of solutions generated for the Shoplifting Problem.

1. give discounts to customers reporting shoplifters
2. use qualifying standards to enter the store
3. convert stores to a buying club
4. develop psychological profiles of shoplifters
5. use exploding dye on certain items of merchandise
6. require checking of coats and packages at store entrance
7. use subliminal, anti-shoplifting messages in store music
8. train clerks to spot potential shoplifters
9. develop public educational programs for the media
10. offer incentives for return of stolen merchandise
11. establish a bartering unit in each store
12. increase the number of security personnel in the stores
13. install electronic detection devices
14. put all merchandise in controlled-access display cases
15. install an electric field around merchandise
16. convert stores to catalog sales
17. install visible cameras to scan frequent shoplifting areas
18. offer free counseling to shoplifters who turn themselves in
19. stage mock arrests of store personnel posing as shoplifters
20. put on a monthly "Shoplifter's Day" to expose arrest records of prior shoplifters
21. offer discounts to participants in shoplifting educational programs if the incidence of shoplifting is reduced
22. pay money to customers reporting shoplifters
23. sell only large, expensive types of merchandise
24. require customers to ask to see merchandise
25. install a one-way mirror in the ceiling for store personnel to watch customers
26. put merchandise in boxes that require a lever to be pushed to open the boxes; once the lever is pushed, personnel are alerted on a TV monitor
27. staple tags onto merchandise; the tags must be electronically neutralized before merchandise can be taken out of the store without sounding an alarm
28. assign code numbers to customers to use in opening display cases

(Continued on page 184).

Figure 11.3 Continued.

29. order merchandise in the store by a phone equipped with a voice-stress analyzer; any indication of anxiety requires assistance of a clerk
30. merchandise above a certain price requires assistance of a clerk
31. install a photo-electric beam above merchandise that sets off an alarm if broken
32. use an alarm that is set off by sound vibrations if merchandise is carried out of the store
33. use a timing device that sets off an alarm hidden in merchandise if not turned off by a clerk
34. hypnotize previous shoplifters so they won't steal again
35. use a combination credit/security card to enter store, unlock display cases, and purchase merchandise; require security check to obtain card
36. spread any price increases arising from shoplifting among convicted shoplifters
37. change store policy so that potential customers must volunteer to undergo a security check to shop without interference of security precautions
38. secure small appliances with screws
39. have merchandise rotate in a controlled-access display case
40. require store clerks to turn switch to open a display case
41. tie down merchandise with nylon lines
42. form a local merchants' commmittee to study the problem
43. use "shock" probation programs

The highest-rated solutions within the categories then might be combined with some solutions from other categories to define the final approach to the problem.

7. Avoiding Surprises

For purposes of illustration, the customer-involvement solutions will be used to respond to the questions in this section.

a. One major obstacle would be overcoming a social taboo on reporting the misdeeds of other people. Another obstacle would be the difficulty involved in establishing the validity of shoplifting claims made by one customer against another.

Figure 11.4 Categorization of Shoplifting Problem solutions.

Category	Solution Number
I. Customer involvement	1, 22
II. Psychological aspects of shoplifting	4, 7, 8, 10, 11, 17, 18, 34
III. Keep shoplifters out of the store	2, 3, 16, 35, 37
IV. Make shoplifting difficult/ prevent from leaving the store	5, 6, 12, 13, 14, 15, 17, 23, 24, 25, 26, 27, 28, 29, 30, 31, 32, 33, 35, 38, 39, 40, 41
V. Educational efforts	9, 19, 20, 21, 36, 42, 43

		Satisfaction				
Criteria	Importance	I	II	III	IV	V
success	5	3 15	3 15	5 25	5 25	1 5
sales	5	2 10	4 20	4 20	5 25	1 5
cost	4	4 16	1 4	2 8	1 4	3 12
customer relations	4	5 20	3 12	1 4	1 4	5 20
time	3	3 9	2 6	1 3	2 6	2 6
physical changes	3	5 15	2 6	3 9	2 6	1 3
implementation	2	4 8	3 6	2 4	1 2	2 4
		93	69	73	72	55

Questions *b.* through *e.* can be responded to best by constructing a chart of potential problems, preventive actions, and ratings of the likelihood (L) and seriousness of occurrence (S) of the problems (1 = not very likely, 5 = very likely; 1 = not very serious, 5 = very serious).

Problems	L	S	Preventive Actions
Unjust accusations	4	5	Develop clear guidelines; mail literature to customers.
Court cases require customer presence	2	3	Use depositions.
Reluctance to accuse others of shoplifting	4	5	Use educational programs and financial incentives.
Shoplifters seek vengeance against accusers	2	5	Use an anonymous reporting procedure; guarantee confidentiality.

f. Some of the major implementation steps would include promotional mailings to customers and newspaper articles to acquaint people with the proposed program, conducting a survey to define the amount of interest in the program, consultations with legal counsel, discussions with company financial personnel regarding the amount of financial investments involved and likely return on investments, development of program brochures, development of program policies, and planning the promotional activities.
g. All current and potential customers, all management personnel, and those persons who would be involved directly with the legal and financial aspects of the program.
h. Perhaps the greatest benefit to be expected from this program would be its value as a public relations and educational device. The program would show customers the store is concerned about the problem and is interested in holding down prices. In addition, the program would help educate the public about the seriousness and pervasiveness of the

problem. Of course, the final outcome should be a slight increase in profits for the store.

i. Time will be the major resource needed to implement and carry through the program. The initial financial costs most likely can be written off against the eventual increase in gains due to less shoplifting.

j. In addition to some of the problems discussed previously, a major problem could be an initial mobbing of the store as people try to spot shoplifters. Some violations of individual rights could occur during the start-up phase. Some problem-solving efforts will be required to deal with these problems.

k. Customers will be rewarded financially and perhaps by a sense of well-being in helping to deal with a social problem. Store personnel will be rewarded by the expectation of increased sales (more customers should come to the store) and profits.

l. The major follow-up activities will be making provisions for handling any court cases that might arise, adjudicating disputes among customers, continued training of store personnel (especially clerks), continued promotion of the program, reporting of the results to the public, and close monitoring of the program, especially during the early stages.

SOME CLOSING THOUGHTS

There are, of course, no guarantees that following this problem solving process will resolve all your problems. (If there were, I'd be living in a tropical resort most of the year and thinking of creative ways to spend all my money.) However, if you have integrated the basic creative thinking concepts in this book, and if you have attempted to apply them to your problems, the outcome should be better than more haphazard approaches. Moreover, you also should feel more confident in your ability to resolve unstructured problems and more satisfied with the results.

If you've learned only one thing from reading this book, it should be that you are a unique, creative individual. Continue thinking that while training your mind every day, and you should have a more fulfilling life. Happy training!

Bibliography & References

Adams, J. L. **Conceptual blockbusting** (2nd ed.). NY: W. W. Norton & Company, 1979.

Albrecht, K. **Brain power.** Englewood Cliffs, NJ: Prentice-Hall, Inc., 1980.

Anderson, B. F. **The complete thinker.** Englewood Cliffs, NJ: Prentice-Hall, Inc., 1980.

Brightman, H. J. **Problem solving: A logical and creative approach.** Atlanta, GA: College of Business Administration, Georgia State University, 1980.

Campbell, D. **Take the road to creativity and get off your dead end.** Niles, IL: Argus Communications, 1977.

Edwards, B. **Drawing on the right-side of the brain.** Los Angeles, CA: J. P. Tarcher, Inc., 1979.

Elijah, A. M. **Thinking unlimited.** Pune, India: Institute of Creative Development, 1980.

Hanks, K., Belliston, L. & Edwards, D. **Design yourself!** Los Altos, CA: William Kaufmann, Inc., 1978.

Hermann, W. E. **The Hermann Brain Dominance Instrument.** Stamford, CT: Applied Creative Services, 1980.

Jacobson, E. **Progressive relaxation.** Chicago, IL: The University of Chicago Press, Midway Reprint, 1974.

Kirst, W. & Diekmeyer, U. **Creativity training.** NY: Peter H. Wyden, Inc., 1973.

Koberg, D. & Bagnall, J. **The universal traveler.** Los Altos, CA: William Kaufmann, Inc., 1976.

Loch, C. How to feed your brain and develop your creativity. *Writer's Digest,* 1981 (February), 20-28.

Lynch, D. The case for disorderly conduct: How to get the most out of managerial manpower. *Management Review,* 1980 (February), 15-19.

Lynch, D. It's time we give the brain its due. *Journal of Organizational Communication*, 1981, 1, 8-10.

Olson, R. W. **The art of creative thinking.** NY: Barnes & Noble, 1980.

Perkins, D. **The mind's best work.** Cambridge, MA: Harvard University Press, 1981.

Prince, G. Putting the other half of the brain to work. *Training,* 1978 (November), 57-58, 60-61.

Raudsepp, E. (with Hough, G. P., Jr.). **Creative growth games.** NY: Jove Publications, Inc., 1977.

Raudsepp, E. **More creative growth games.** NY: Perigee Books, 1980.

Raudsepp, E. How creative are you? In *Dun's Review,* Business probes the creative spark, 1980 (January), 32-38.

Samuels, M. & Samuels, N. **Seeing with the mind's eye.** NY: Random House, Inc., 1975.

Simberg, A. L. **Creativity at work.** Boston, MA: Industrial Education Institute, 1964.

Torrance, E. P. **The Torrance Tests of Creative Thinking.** Lexington, MA: Personnel Press/Ginn, 1974.

VanGundy, A. B. **Techniques of structured problem solving** (2nd ed.). NY: Van Nostrand Reinhold, 1988.

Wujec, T. **Pumping ions, games and exercises to flex your mind.** Garden City, NY: Doubleday & Company, 1988.

Index

Recommended Readings . . .

Stalking The Wild Solution
by Arthur B. VanGundy, Ph.D.
ISBN 0-943456-19-3 194 pages $12.95

Most problem-solving specialists recognize that a high quality solution rarely results without adequate problem identification and analysis. However, most of us have been conditioned to be solution-minded, not problem-minded. We want to propose solutions before we have a proper understanding of our problems.

The book is divided into two parts. The first part introduces the general problem-finding process, discusses other problem-solving approaches, and describes an eight-part typology for categorizing problems along an ill-structured to well-structured continuum. The second part uses a hunting metaphor to describe such activities as sensing problutions, developing a strategic approach, and techniques for data gathering and refining problem understanding.

The Creative Mind
by Frederic Flach, M.D.
ISBN 0-943456-27-4 370 pages $19.95

We live in an age of upheaval. Knowledge of ourselves and of the universe is expanding at a geometric rate. Creativity has always been at the heart of mankind's ability to cope, survive and evolve. Perhaps never before has an *understanding of the creative process* been so essential to attain these goals.

It was with this purpose in mind that **Frederic Flach, M.D.** (author of **Resilience: Discovering A New Strength At Times Of Stress**) originally compiled and edited a series of monographs for the psychiatric community. Now in book form, this collection of priceless viewpoints about the creative process and its relationship to human behavior is available for general distribution.

The publication is a major reference for those interested in the nature of the creative process and the many facets of professional and human enterprise based on it.

Risking Change: Endings & Beginnings
by William F. Sturner, Ph.D.
ISBN 0-943456-20-7 162 Pages $12.95

This book analyzes each facet of the risk taking process. It offers a unique blend of analyses, models and applications presented in a clear, concise and usable format. The many examples and diagrams will help readers identify their own traits and behaviors, understand the interplay between risk-taking and psychological needs, and anticipate the risks involved in each stage of individual development.

Calculated Risk: Stratagies For Managing Change
by William F. Sturner, Ph.D.
ISBN 0-943456-26-6 273 pages $18.95

This companion workbook to the above title features a wide array of inventories, questionnaires, analyses, and experimental exercises designed to help readers understand the impact of risk taking on their personal relationships, work arenas, and personal growth. Insighting, affirmations, and action planning will assist readers in taking that "calculated risk," design concrete strategies, and achieve their goals.

Key Issues In Creativity, Innovation & Entrepreneurship
by Bruce G. Whiting, Ph.D. & George T. Solomon, Ph.D.
ISBN 0-943456-32-0 202 pages $12.95

People who are in the profession of observing American businesses continually cite creativity, innovation and entrepreneurship – alone or in combination – as the key elements for economic success in the 1990s and beyond.

In this book, the authors bring together the viewpoints of some nationally-known experts and successful practitioners in each behavior. Some of the views examine the similarities and overlapping attributes while others amplify the differences among these behaviors. Collectively, they lead to a deeper understanding of how these critical behaviors occur...and how they will effect our collective future.